Almost Perfect

Almost Perfect

Diane Daniels Manning

ISBN 978-0692338193

Dedicated to:

All special children and their families
and
Therapy pets, the official ones and the natural-born amateurs

Contents

Chapter 1

More than anything in the world, Benny Neusner wanted his mother to be proud of him, and next after that, he wanted a dog. He hadn't given up on his mom, but a dog was out of the question. No matter how hard he begged for one, his dad and stepmother always refused. They'd had the same old fight again this morning at breakfast.

"A boy who hides his homework in a pizza box isn't ready for a dog," Sonya had chirped with a satisfied smile.

"Your stepmother's right," his dad agreed. "I expect a 90 in math, or at least an 80, before I even think about getting you a dog."

Benny could never get grades like that. He was different from the other kids at his therapeutic school who were a bunch of brains. The teachers were kind and gave him special work to do, but school wasn't his thing. A dog was. A dog would be company when his dad and Sonya left him home alone. A dog would be someone to play with when his mother had to miss one of their visits. A dog would understand how it felt to be lonely.

The sky was growing dark, and all the other students had left school for home hours ago. He decided his mother must have been tied up on important business and wasn't coming after all. He slung his backpack over his shoulder and headed for home. The deserted, country road made him wish even more that he had a dog alongside him for company. His dad's only neighbor for a quarter mile in each direction was an old woman who lived in a big Victorian mansion, and what good was that? What could they possibly have in common?

Every few minutes, he stopped for a little rest and tipped back his head, hoping to see the special star he and his mother used to watch together. He had learned in science class that the star was really a planet, but he liked to imagine his mother was staring at it, too, thinking about him and all the good times they used to have together.

He had almost reached the bottom of his dad's driveway when a cloud moved and his mother's star appeared. And at that very moment he heard it: a puppy crying! At least it might be a puppy. He wanted a dog so badly he was afraid he had only imagined it. Not that he heard voices in his head, human or animal. Dr. Kate, the school's principal and his shrink, had told him before that he wasn't nuts, just a little mixed up on account of the crazy life he had been living so far. Sometimes he acted young for fourteen, but like Dr. Kate said, a boy with so much on his mind burns up a lot of brain power.

He fished around the bottom of his backpack for a flashlight and an extra granola bar before he remembered he had polished it off with a box of Oreos and a carton of juice while waiting for his mother. He patted his little paunch and wished he had saved a couple of cookies, but at least he found the flashlight. He tossed the backpack into the bushes where his comics would be safe and hurried on. The weatherman had predicted a blizzard before Christmas, too dangerous for a little fellow to be alone outside without his mother.

The crying seemed to be coming from the direction of the old woman's house. He would need to climb the stone fence that separated her property from his dad's and walk across a couple of fields to get there. He might not make it home in time for dinner, but this could be his best chance for a dog. He had to find out.

He picked up the pace and didn't notice something sticking out from under a pile of dried leaves until he stubbed his toe. He pointed the flashlight. The sign must have been lying there a long time because the words were mostly hidden by some awful-looking green stuff. He found a small branch and scraped off the slime. His eyes grew wide. Someone had painted the picture of a poodle with a fancy haircut and the words "Umpawaug Kennels, Redding, Connecticut. Elizabeth Rutledge, Breeder/Owner."

He slapped his head with an open palm. How could he have missed something as important as a kennel right next door? Even though he had only been living with his dad and Sonya for three months, he took a lot of pride in knowing what was happening around him. Whenever he relaxed and didn't pay attention, things boomeranged on him. Elizabeth Rutledge, whoever she was, should be more careful and not leave signs lying around where people could stumble over them.

He checked the picture again. One thing was for sure: the puppy had better not be a poodle. His dad wouldn't let him have a dog — period! — but especially not a poodle. His dad said poodles were sissy dogs, and his dad was right. He had a book with pictures of every kind of dog in the world and had already picked out his favorite: a brown and white beagle like Snoopy. He wouldn't mind a collie like Lassie, either. A collie might rescue someone from a terrible tragedy, like falling through the ice and drowning. The same thing almost happened to him last winter, but it turned out to be a really deep pothole. Even a dog from the pound would be fine with him, but not one time did he think a poodle with a goofy-looking hairdo was the dog for him.

He fixed his eyes on the old woman's turret as a guidepost, and a few minutes later, he climbed over the stone wall onto her property. Rows and rows of kennels with empty dog runs were silhouetted in the moonlight like a city empty of life. Goosebumps rose on his flesh, and he started to back away when he heard crying again. The sound was coming from inside a small white building behind the old woman's house.

He gathered his courage. He had come this far; he might as well finish. He spotted a small window and shined his flashlight through it. The light bounced off the wall and revealed a room that was a mess, even by teenage standards. Crates for carting dogs were scattered around the floor with their doors hanging open. A counter stacked with old magazines lined the far wall. A deep sink like a school janitor's stood at the end. On shelves above the counter, dozens and dozens of silver trophies, some with statues of poodles, were stacked in neat rows like forgotten soldiers waiting for orders.

He moved the flashlight, and this time he noticed a door on the opposite side of the shed. It swung back and forth on its hinges, making an eerie, creaking noise he might have mistaken for a puppy. He listened again. No, the sound wasn't the door, and it wasn't a puppy. A person was crying, maybe a boy even. Whoever it was, their heart was breaking.

Cautiously, he walked around the shed and stepped through the door. Now that he was inside, his flashlight illuminated a dark corner it couldn't reach through the window. He discovered a sort of stall, only shorter, that might have been meant for a pony. A pony wasn't a dog, but it wasn't bad. He tiptoed closer and pulled the latch. A ghastly squeak pierced the silence, and some awful-tasting stuff lurched up from his stomach.

The crying stopped and a gravelly voice croaked from

inside the stall, "Whoever you are, you're trespassing on private property."

Scared as he was, he couldn't stand not knowing. He peered over the side of the stall. A battery-operated lantern illuminated an old woman hunched over on a three-legged stool. Her bathrobe, if that's what it was, had ridden up over her knobby knees, and her curly gray hair stuck out every which way, like she had been running her fingers through it.

"You heard me, boy," she growled. "State your business."

His mouth was so dry he didn't think he could squeeze out a word, but he managed to say, "I heard a noise."

She gave her eyes a hasty wipe and stuffed a crumpled tissue in her pocket. "Noise?" she asked, her scratchy voice full of doubt.

"Sorry, ma'am, my mistake."

He backed away slowly, hoping to make an uneventful getaway, but she had already lost interest in him. She muttered soft words he couldn't quite make out and beckoned to something hidden in the corner. Curious, he pointed his flashlight over her shoulder.

His jaw dropped. "A dog!"

Chapter 2

Benny had been expecting a puppy, not a full-grown dog like the one looking up at him with kind, almond-shaped eyes. It was about three feet tall at the crown and sported a warm, chestnut-colored coat. No puffed-out mane or pom-pom bracelets like the dog on the sign, just a short bobbed tail and a fluffy topknot that practically made his fingers itch he wanted to touch it so badly. "I'm glad he's not a poodle," he said, stepping closer.

She circled her arm around the dog's neck protectively, as if afraid he had come to steal it. Still, her words were calm enough. "Not he — she, and Susie's a poodle all right. About to become a mother any time now, maybe even Christmas Day. That's why she's in the whelping pen."

"You mean Susie's having puppies?"

She nodded, and for a moment, he thought she might start crying again. "It's her first litter. That's why I'm out here in the puppy shed checking on her."

"I've been wanting a puppy," he said, his voice choked with longing. "Maybe they won't all be poodles."

"They'll all be poodles. I made sure of that."

He wondered if the poodle on the sign was the father. He gave Susie another look. "She doesn't look that much like a poodle," he said.

"For your information," she said, straightening her

spine, "large poodles like Susie here are called standard poodles. They're hunting dogs, like a Lab or a golden retriever, if you know what they are."

He nodded. "Oh, yes, ma'am. I have a dog book. No funny haircuts."

She sucked in a breath and spoke through her teeth like she had given this speech a hundred times. "The funny haircut, as you call it, is for show poodles. It's required by the judge. Umpawaug Kennels' poodles are famous all over the world. People you see on TV every day insist on them — even politicians."

He pointed at Susie resting her chin comfortably on the old woman's shoulder. "She doesn't look bad for a poodle. No pom-poms."

"Susie's show days are behind her. Mine, too. I'm retiring, selling off the dogs and closing the kennel."

"If you're retiring, why is Susie having puppies?"

She twitched like a flea had bitten her. "They're not mine. I sold Susie awhile back. Her new owner tripped on a tennis ball one of the dogs left lying about and broke her wrist. I'm helping her out."

"You wouldn't be Elizabeth Rutledge by any chance?" he asked. "I saw the sign."

"That's me, but you can call me Bess. Everyone does. And you?"

He closed the middle button on his school shirt that had popped open and straightened his jacket. "Benny, Benny Neusner. I live in the brick house over there." He pointed with his thumb in the direction of his dad's.

She squinted up at him, as if trying to decide if she'd met him before. "Say, shouldn't you be in school or something?"

He jerked back his head. Even Sonya wouldn't make him go to school in the middle of the night. "You don't know much about kids, do you?"

She looked down. "No, not much. At least about boys."

A shadow crossed her face, and he was afraid he'd said the wrong thing. "Come to think of it, I don't know much about old people. I never had a grandmother, at least not one I knew in person, and I'm kind of glad. A mother and a stepmother are plenty."

He decided this was as good a time as any to leave, but before he could make his escape, the door squeaked open and a second large dog stuck its head inside. Its fuzzy coat was the color of warm beach sand, and its kind, intelligent eyes looked trustingly into Benny's.

Bess pushed herself up off the stool, her knees cracking with the effort. "Champion Umpawaug McCreery," she introduced, "the world's top producer of champion standard poodles. He's the puppies' father."

McCreery raised his chin a little higher and held his tail in its full upright position.

"No wonder you're proud of him. I can't imagine a better honor than being the world's greatest stud," he said, but he detected a note of sadness behind her bragging, like she had missed out on something important, or maybe McCreery had.

Her eyes flicked to the shelves full of silver trophies. "Producing great puppies isn't the only honor McCreery has behind him. In his day, he won every important dog show there is." She hesitated and added in a whisper, "Except *the* one."

Tears welled up in her eyes, and he was afraid she might start crying again. Nothing made him feel worse than an unhappy grownup. He knew better than to ask questions, so he held out his hand to McCreery instead.

The big dog ambled toward him, each step falling lightly in spite of his size. He sat in front of Benny and stuck out his paw. Benny grabbed it and shook it up and down. McCreery jumped up on his hind legs, tail whirring, and tugged the boy's sleeve in an invitation to play. Benny laughed and hugged McCreery around the neck as if he would never let go. The big dog pranced on his hind feet, sweeping the boy along like they were partners at a fancy dress ball.

Benny turned to the old woman with a grin full of braces. "I don't care if he's a poodle. I'll take him."

She signaled the dog to her side and drew him in close. "I'm sorry. McCreery's not for sale."

Benny flushed. "Not for sale? But you said you're getting rid of your dogs."

She stood. "Not McCreery. Never!"

McCreery, a worried frown between his eyes, moved to her side. She stroked his head. It seemed to calm them both.

Benny felt sorry for the old woman, but what about him? He had been waiting all his life for a dog like McCreery. He didn't care what his father said or anyone else. He wouldn't give him up. He started to tell the old woman so when McCreery moved off silently. He and Susie stood nose to nose, sharing dog secrets. Susie yawned, circled in place, and lowered herself onto the soft bedding.

In his mind's eye, Benny saw newborn puppies snuggling against Susie's belly, taking in their breakfast. One little brown fellow, the miniature of his father, was pushing his legs against the others. McCreery looked down on them all, guarding his family: mother and father together with their little boy.

Benny balled up his fists. It wasn't fair. It really wasn't. No way could he break up a family, not even a dog's. He dropped to his knees in front of McCreery.

With a whimper, McCreery looked back and forth between Benny and Bess. He nuzzled Benny's chin, then turned and leaned against Bess.

Benny wiped his nose on his sleeve and slowly got to his feet. "Good-bye, McCreery. I'll never forget you." He turned and ran into the night.

Chapter 3

Bess hung up the phone and leaned heavily against the kitchen counter. She scowled at the cheerful sun streaming through the window and yanked down the shade. Thankfully, her sister Mona was still upstairs getting her beauty rest. She needed time to prepare herself for what lay ahead and didn't feel like answering a lot of questions that wouldn't change her mind.

Strange that with all she was facing today, she had fallen asleep thinking about the boy with the fine sandy hair and baby smooth cheeks she'd met in the puppy shed last night. His open, honest face and crescent moon smile when he spotted McCreery didn't fit with his deep, sad eyes. She couldn't think where she had seen eyes like that before — besides in her own mirror this morning. He seemed familiar, like a memory she couldn't grab hold of, but of what? Perhaps it was only the way he had reacted to McCreery. She had observed the scene hundreds of times and knew what it meant. He had lost his heart to the big guy. More surprising was McCreery's reaction. McCreery was friendly, but he wasn't a golden retriever that never met a stranger.

She hated to disappoint the boy, but there was no way she could give up McCreery. Like she'd said, he was hers for life. She would have gladly let the boy have one of Susie's and McCreery's puppies instead. She was entitled to pick of the litter, so she could make it happen, but he wasn't interested. Even if he was, it would be another three months before the puppies would be ready to go, and he didn't seem like the type who could wait.

She sighed and pushed those thoughts away. If she kept on like this, she would never get through what lay ahead today. She stuck her head in the refrigerator and discovered the plastic milk container was nearly empty. She tipped the dregs into her mouth and tossed the bottle into the trash. In the old days, the milkman left glass bottles topped with thick, yellow cream on the doorstep. Now, Burritt's Dairy had been turned into a farm museum so school children could learn what Redding was like fifty years ago, before it got transformed into an ex-urban retreat for New York commuters.

She placed her hand on the doorknob to let in McCreery and automatically stuck out her foot to block a bunch of curious puppies bent on escaping. For a moment, she had forgotten. For the first time in nearly half a century, there were no puppies. An unfamiliar tightness gripped her heart like an overwound rubber band, but at least she had McCreery.

She opened the door and banged on a metal dog dish with a spoon. A moment passed, and she banged again. Still no McCreery. Her breath caught in her throat. Could the lovesick boy have snuck back and stolen him? It had happened more than once to valuable show dogs.

Before the terrible thought could take hold, a flash of grinning teeth and fifty pounds of curly brown coat trimmed in a lamb's cut rounded the corner with his lush ears flying. Even at ten years old, the last of the Umpawaug champions was everything a standard poodle ought to be: alert, fun-loving, graceful.

McCreery rubbed his face against her leg in greeting and moved to investigate his dinner bowl. Reassured, she poured his breakfast kibbles into a ceramic bowl decorated with poodles in various colors and poses, a Christmas gift from her son, David, years ago. The dry pellets hitting the bottom sounded overly loud in the oversized Victorian kitchen where a large staff once prepared enormous meals for a growing family. The cracked linoleum floor, the moss green cabinets with glass doors, and the wooden table with spindle legs were the same as when the house had been built. Only the chef-quality stove and shiny copper pots were new. Mona had brought them with her last summer when she sold the house Benny lived in now and announced she was staying with her — temporarily — until her condo in Florida was ready. So far, she showed no sign of leaving. The mere thought of it made Bess shudder even if she would rather die than admit it, especially to her sister, but her twin was standing in the doorway and had seen.

"Are you all right?" Mona asked, permitting herself a rare frown. She had been avoiding wrinkles since her twenties. Even at this early hour, she wore open-toed mules with two-inch heels and an aubergine scarf that trailed behind her. Her tinted hair was perfectly coiffed.

McCreery lifted his head, sniffing Mona's familiar aroma of vanilla and lilacs, and looked back and forth between the sisters, trying to decide if Mona's concern was more than the twins' usual sparring.

"Why wouldn't I be? In fact, I'm more than fine. I just finished phoning the man with the backhoe. He'll be here in a few minutes." For a moment, the shocked look on her sister's face almost made up for the knot in her chest.

Mona held up her palms as if to block her twin's disastrous choice. "You can't. Umpawaug is the top kennel for poodles in America. You've spent a lifetime building it, not that I would have chosen that life for myself," she added with a tug at her scarf.

Bess crossed her arms over her chest. "Well, if that isn't

just like you. For years you've been telling me ladies like us weren't brought up to raise a bunch of smelly dogs — not that poodles smell, mind you — and now that I'm retiring, you're first in line to criticize." McCreery padded over and pushed his nose under her elbow. For once, she ignored him.

Mona's artfully made-up face collapsed. She swallowed and forced out the difficult words. "I was wrong, Bessie. Of the two of us, you were the one who found what she wanted in life. I was too jealous to see it."

A smile flickered at the corners of Bess's mouth. "You, Mona? Jealous?"

Mona rose and tossed the end of her scarf over her shoulder. "Oh, for heaven's sake!" She lit the gas stove, cracked an egg into a frying pan, and turned, face flushed with self-satisfaction. "It's a good thing you let Hannah Washington use McCreery with Susie. I admit I was against it at the time, but at least you'll have pick of the litter. You don't need a whole kennel for one little puppy." She raised her chin imperiously, signaling the grave sacrifice she was about to make. "You can keep it right here in the kitchen. I won't say a word."

Her twin's kind intentions finally penetrated Bess's carefully crafted armor, and the truth escaped. She dropped into a chair. "No more puppies, Mona," she said, her voice cracking in spite of herself. "I'm too old."

McCreery gave a faint whimper and placed his front paws on her lap. She wove her fingers through his curly brown topknot.

Mona stomped her foot. "Nonsense! If you're too old, then so am I, and that's ridiculous." She paused, studying her twin over the bridge of her nose. "Too old for what, if I may ask?"

The answer came in a whisper. "To take a dog into the show ring myself. Standard poodles are big dogs, or haven't you noticed? The handler has to be able to keep up so the dog can show off his stride."

Mona flashed her loveliest smile, slid the egg onto a plate, and sat. "Is that all? You can hire one of those handler people. Isn't that what Hannah and the rest of them do?"

Bess waved the idea away like a pesky fly. Mona didn't know that Hannah's club foot, well-disguised as it was by special shoes, prevented her from showing a dog to its best advantage. "Sorry, that's not for me. I've never hired a handler, and it's too late to start now."

Mona took a quick peek at her reflection in the toaster and pulled her scarf back around. "I'm sorry you feel that way. You don't hear me whining or letting myself go because of a few little inconveniences."

Bess swallowed a sigh. "What if I got in the ring and my asthma kicked in or my trick knee gave out, and I landed flat on my face? Would that be fair to the dog? To me? I'd rather Hannah give the puppies the show careers they deserve."

Mona wrinkled her nose. "There's something you're not admitting. Old age would never stop a person like you. At least please explain why you're selling the puppies to Hannah, of all people. You two were always at each other's throats, trying to one-up one another."

Bess sighed. Mona would never understand why Hannah was the only sensible choice. A beautiful, trusting face was Umpawaug's signature contribution to the breed and the trait most easily lost through careless breeding. In spite of old wounds between them, Hannah was the one person on earth who would keep the distinctive expression alive.

"And what about a good home for the dogs — and love?" Mona added, pulling out all the stops.

"Hannah will love them," Bess said in a whisper. "Don't you think I considered that above everything?" She met her sister's eyes. "I'm finished, Mona. No more dogs."

McCreery rose on his hind legs and circled her face with curious sniffs, like a person reading Braille. "Don't worry, big fella. I didn't mean you." She gave him a quick hug and rose stiffly. She poured the remains of her cereal into his bowl and turned toward the door.

Mona knew without words what her twin intended to do. She stood. "I'll go with you."

Bess shook her head, unable to speak. She reached for the pea jacket hanging on a hook beside the back door and slipped her arms through the sleeves. A wool scarf with worn-down tassels stuck out one end. With a determined yank, Bess pulled it out and hung it around her neck. She took a deep breath and opened the door. McCreery grabbed his favorite toy, a pink and lime stuffed fish, and slipped through the opening ahead of her.

The cold, humid air seeped under her cuffs and down her neck. She imagined the long, dreary winter ahead and wondered whether it might not be better to postpone the inevitable until spring. The whole world would seem more hopeful then.

Before she could change her mind, the wind caught the loose end of her scarf and whipped it across her cheek like a slap. Its sting snapped her back to reality. Why did she doubt the choice she had vehemently defended to Mona just moments ago? She knew the answer. Her argument was a child's popsicle-stick fort held together with cheap glue. Now that her sister wasn't around to argue the opposite point of view, her locked-up fears threatened to escape. Yes, she probably could manage one new puppy. Yes, she was tempted. Yes, she could hire someone to help socialize him, maybe even that strange boy Benny. But no, she could never let a handler take her dog into the ring. Showing dogs wasn't a job; it was a passion. If she couldn't do it herself, her heart wouldn't be in it. Now was the time to stop.

McCreery himself had no such gloomy thoughts.

Oblivious to the destination and the task before them, he ran ahead in circles, raring to go wherever she took him. They passed rows of empty kennels, each with its own individual dog run, where as many as a dozen standard poodles once made up the Umpawaug Empire. Every few seconds he looked back, making sure she was still behind him. Then he disappeared from sight behind a thick clump of laurel bushes.

A chill ran down her spine, and it came to her in a flash, like to someone drowning, how empty her life would be without him. What if she gave up everything else today and ended up losing him, too? She had Mona and her grown son, David, but McCreery was different. He was the one creature on earth she felt completely safe with.

A moment later, he reappeared. She signaled him to her side, hiding her relief, and he followed her to the puppy shed. She opened the door and he dashed in ahead not even stopping to greet Susie in the whelping pen. He sniffed the room curiously, trying to figure out why they were there. The faint odor coming off his mistress told him heartache lay ahead. He dropped his toy and stood with his paws on the ledge, ears alert.

The sound of a powerful engine churning up gravel and road debris reached their ears moments before the backhoe appeared. McCreery pressed against Bess' side, eyes dark with worry riveted on her face. Her hand dropped automatically and stroked his head. He was the one she usually shared her feelings with, not that she was very good at it even with him, but today a different dog might have been better. One who didn't share so many memories. One who didn't know her so well.

The backhoe was almost at the top of the driveway.

She tipped back her head and cleared her throat. McCreery recognized the sound and nuzzled his head under her hand. Together they watched the backhoe cut across the driveway toward the rows of silent kennels. She turned away before the first crunch of the blade against wood. Before the morning was over, all that was left of Umpawaug Kennels was a barren field and a puppy shed empty of life.

Chapter 4

Benny sat alone on the school's front porch. All the other kids had driven off with their parents right after the last note of the holiday concert had been sung, eager to begin the two-week vacation. He could have gotten a ride home with his dad and Sonya, but he was still hoping. His mother hadn't actually promised, but she said she would try. She could have had a flat tire or gotten stuck behind a freight train at the railroad crossing in Bethel, and think how sad she would be if he wasn't there waiting. She would never disappoint him this close to Christmas. This year she would give him something special for sure. Maybe the cool new game he had hinted about the last time he saw her. Maybe a puppy.

Thinking about a puppy made him remember meeting his dream dog last night, and his mouth turned down at the corners. Bess should have given him McCreery like he wanted. Big dogs needed a lot of exercise, and she was too old to run around and play. Not that he was crazy about working up a sweat himself, but McCreery and he could have had a great time curled up on his bed reading Spiderman comics together.

He polished off the last of the tree-shaped cookies with red and green sprinkles he had stuffed in his pocket and was about to leave when the sound of a car turning into the school driveway stopped him. It wasn't his mother. This engine was purring like a well-fed cat. A black stretch limo glided to a stop at the front steps. Before the liveried chauffeur could come around and open the rear door, a girl about his own age stepped out. Her mother, or whoever she was, waited inside. The girl hurried onto the porch, not stopping to admire the tall white columns, and rushed past him. She picked a window and pressed her nose against the cool glass as if her whole future was hidden inside.

He considered it his duty to know everything that happened at his school, and if the girl was a new student, it was big news. From the way she was dressed, she was probably an escapee from a British boarding school. He had never actually seen anyone wear brown oxfords with flaps and knee-high wool stockings before, except in the movies. On second thought, she might be French. All those Frenchies wore berets with striped ribbons down the back. Or was it Scottish people? That would account for the short kilt she was wearing even though it was practically freezing outside.

He spat on his hand, slicked back the fine, sandy bangs that hung limply over his forehead and tried to remember if people from Scotland spoke English. He tapped the girl on the shoulder. "Can I help you?"

The girl whirled around and answered in perfect American English, "Not really. My mother enrolled me here for next semester, and I wanted to check it out."

He nodded approvingly. "I'm Benny Neusner. School's closed for two weeks, but I can fill you in on everything you want to know. I'm kind of an expert."

The girl looked him up and down, not exactly curious but not indifferent, either. More like she was acting out what was expected. She stuck out her chin and locked eyes with him. "I'm Steffie and I have Asperger's. You know what that is, right?"

He felt the old anger rise up inside him from all the kids who had called him stupid. Then he remembered it hadn't happened once at New Hope School and unclenched his fists. "I think we studied it in health class once, but I might not have been paying that much attention."

"That's understandable. In case you want to know, Asperger's kids are real smart, can't make friends, and don't make eye contact. You can read all about it in the *DSM.* That's short for *Diagnostic and Statistical Manual.* It's practically my mother's bible.

He nodded. He had seen one plenty of times in Dr. Kate's office. Once, he had even used the thick book to flatten out a homework paper he'd dropped in the toilet by mistake. The print in the book was real small and looked boring.

Steffie tossed her thick, black hair. "Say, you haven't told me what's wrong with you."

He wasn't sure how to take her question. Every student in New Hope School had a reason for being there, but no one went around bragging about it. He was about to tell her it was none of her business, but she was kind of cute, so he said, "I'm working on my temper." He was too embarrassed to tell her he'd been bullied at his old school because it took him longer than most kids to figure stuff out — not everything, mostly just schoolwork.

"Well, don't forget I have Asperger's, so don't expect us to be friends or anything."

He blushed. Being friends was exactly what he had been hoping for, maybe more. Lately he'd been thinking he wouldn't mind having a girlfriend, especially since a dog seemed like a lost cause. "I overheard Dr. Kate telling one of the teachers half the students here diagnosed with Asperger's are really just anxious. I was resting up on the waiting room sofa, and they didn't know I was listening."

Her head jerked up, her brown eyes bright with interest.

"Well, I have it. My mother heard about it on one of her programs. *Oprah,* I think. She dragged me to three different shrinks and every single one agreed with her. Two docs didn't even need to meet me to figure it out."

He didn't know what to say. Fortunately, he was saved when Steffie's mother summoned her with a flutter of fingers.

"See you next year," Steffie called as she climbed into the limo.

"Yeah, see ya." He hefted his backpack and headed for home, wondering if Steffie would forget all about him when the other kids came back, or if this time, he might have found a friend for keeps.

Chapter 5

The sky was nearly dark when Mona awoke. She peered at the kitchen clock, disoriented for a moment, not sure what had awakened her. She remembered hearing the final dump truck haul off the dregs of Umpawaug Kennels and watching her sister disappear upstairs beyond the reach of comfort. Overcome by a twin's sympathetic emotions, she must have fallen asleep.

An insistent tapping came again at the back door. McCreery rushed downstairs, ears cocked, body alert, eyes searching. He reached the door ahead of her, pushing his nose through the gap as she pulled it open. A stranger stood on the stoop with an embarrassed smile. His eyes were hidden behind sunglasses, although the sun already had dipped behind the horizon.

"Yes?" she said, glad for McCreery's protection, a thought she recalled later with painful irony.

The man took off his cap and held it respectfully against his chest. "Sorry to bother you, but I seem to have lost my bearings. I'm trying to find Route 53 and must have missed the sign." He took a step closer, and McCreery let out a warning growl. He was a friendly dog, but Mona hadn't given him the signal to relax.

"You're pretty far afield," she said, keeping up her own guard. Redding's roads were a tangle of ancient cow paths, but Route 53 was clearly marked.

"I saw your light and the sign for Umpawaug Kennels," he said. "I'm a bit of an amateur breeder myself." His eyes traveled over McCreery's body with an almost professional air. "Nice looking dog — the famous Umpawaug Champion McCreery, I presume."

Mona wondered how he knew, but before she could ask, he slipped a large dog biscuit out of his pocket and held it out. McCreery quivered with excitement, his suspicions vanquished. He snatched the biscuit out of the man's hand and slipped out the door.

"McCreery, no!" she shouted, gathering her wits. Bess would never allow a stranger to feed anything to her dog. She pushed past him and stared into the empty night. "It's all right," he said. "I have them made special. My poodle Dolly loves them."

Mona barely glanced at him. "Left at the end of the driveway, right at the second stop sign," she said through a clenched jaw.

The man turned, now apparently as eager to leave as she was to be rid of him. Mona shut the door firmly and turned to see Bess staring after him.

"Who was that?" she asked, bending to pick up the toy fish McCreery had dropped by the door.

Mona colored. Perhaps her imagination was working overtime. Too many worries jarred loose by the backhoe and troubling thoughts of her sister's empty days ahead. "Some man looking for Route 53. He gave McCreery a biscuit."

Bess didn't let her finish. A van with a dented right front fender, its engine turned off, rolled silently down the driveway toward Gallows Hill Road. "Stop! Come back!" she shouted, running toward the car. The driver switched on the lights, and the engine sputtered to life. Through the back window, she made out the wires of a dog crate. A pair of helpless eyes stared back at her.

McCreery!

She turned this way and that, arms flailing. She took a step forward and then a step back, as though trapped by indecision. A sharp wind cut across the lawn and rustled the branches of the fourteen-foot pine tree beside the front door. A string of colored Christmas lights jangled like rusty blades in a tin can, flashing on and off. She sank to her knees, a wail rising from deep within her.

It was too late to hunt for the car keys. Even a minute's head start was too much. There were too many forks and side roads he could take. They stood and stared wordlessly at the toy fish lying limp and lifeless where McCreery had dropped it.

Mona phoned the resident state trooper. At first, he didn't think a missing dog was serious police business, but when she explained McCreery's credentials, he remembered other snatchings of well-known show dogs. The trooper asked for a description of the kidnapper, and she told him what she could remember. The man seemed ordinary enough, about forty, medium height, medium weight, medium everything. The only thing that stood out was the van with the dented right fender. It wasn't much to go on.

Mona knew she would never forget the image of McCreery disappearing right in front of her like a magician's trick or forgive herself that he'd been stolen on her watch, but more immediately, she worried her sister wouldn't survive the loss. Bess would go through the motions as long as Susie's puppies needed her, but after that? Even a twin sister couldn't be sure.

Chapter 6

David Rutledge pulled down the bill of his red-and-black checkered cap and bent into the wind. He was heading for his mother's house with two matching packages tucked under his arms. The snow had begun a half hour earlier, and its steady pace promised an old-fashioned white Christmas. The tiny flakes caked his eyelashes, and he was glad he had chosen the shortcut through the empty field that used to house his mother's kennels. If he hadn't sidestepped a rut the backhoe had left behind, he would have missed seeing the small dark mound buried under a half-inch of snow. The object was too small for anything that had once been alive, except maybe a rodent or a migrating bird left behind by its fellows.

Curious, he stepped closer for a better look, and a veneer of ice hidden under the snow caught him by surprise. His long legs slid out from under him, and he landed on his back. He lay still a moment, taking stock. He could wiggle all his fingers and toes, but his Aunt Mona's carefully wrapped present had been crushed at one corner. Inside, a cashmere sweater in his mother's favorite cherry red would be safe; so would Mona's signature emerald green inside Bess's box. Every holiday and birthday since they were children, the twins had traded presents, each afraid the other's was better. After thirty-six years, he had found a solution.

He picked himself up, stomped his boots clean and brushed the snow off his backside. Up ahead, smoke spiraled out of the chimney of his mother's Victorian like a Currier & Ives greeting card. He knew the homey illusion was paper thin, but his throat grew tight, wishing there would be more than the three of them at the Christmas dinner table this year. At least his divorce hadn't left any kids to divide in half over the holidays. He tucked the presents back under his arm and resumed his trek. Whatever the snow had claimed would have to wait.

He trudged on a few feet and turned. If he didn't satisfy his curiosity, the mysterious object would nag him all day. Swiping his eyes with the back of his glove, he gently brushed away the thin layer of snow. He stared for a long moment, uncertain what to do. Then, cupping his hands like a fisherman scooping his catch, he lifted the tiny object. Steadying it against his chest with one hand, he reached into his pocket for the rolled-up newspaper his mother had asked him to bring. He spread the paper out on the snow, gently dropped the object on top, and rolled the newspaper up like a shroud. He stuck the little bundle in his jacket pocket and bent his head into the wind.

Chapter 7

Bess couldn't remember a Christmas storm like this one in all her seventy years, a regular nor'easter that would keep all but the most headstrong indoors. The day suited her mood, but waiting for Susie to whelp in the puppy shed where generations of Umpawaug puppies had been born was no time for negative thoughts. As long as McCreery's puppies needed her, she could manage; but once she had handed them over to Hannah, she was finished with dogs for good. She couldn't take the heartache one more time.

She reached over and gave Susie a reassuring pat on the head. She didn't know when the first puppy would arrive, but decades of experience told her it would be soon. Susie shifted on the bed of shredded newspaper, and Bess checked again. Still no puppy. From what she could tell by palpating Susie's belly, it would be a good-sized litter.

"You played in the snow a long time this morning," she told the young mother-to-be. "Even a St. Bernard would have whined to come inside. If I hadn't marked off the days since the breeding and taken your temperature, who knows where those puppies would've been born?"

The thought gave her a sudden jolt. She pushed Susie gently to one side. Just as she suspected, Susie had whelped her first puppy without the slightest fuss or bother: a robust black boy, wet and shiny. Susie needed to break open the sack so the puppy could breathe.

"Good girl, go on, lick," she urged, but Susie was already following nature's instincts. Back during the first whelping at Umpawaug Kennels, she had been pathetically ignorant of the process, but, mercifully, the new mother delivered her puppies safely. The experience made her the first to volunteer whenever a neophyte breeder needed help. Hannah was just one of many. That's how they had met. Her chief rival had once been her protégé.

Bess waited another minute while mother and son finished their introductions. Then she picked up the puppy and held him up to the light in both hands. She counted twenty little pinpricks of toenails and nodded approvingly at the ripples where his black coat promised to grow in thick and strong. She placed him gently on a food scale and weighed and measured him, jotting down his vital statistics in a well-worn spiral notebook. She couldn't remember how many more were stored in file boxes. Every puppy born at Umpawaug Kennels had been recorded the same way. She imagined Hannah kept everything on computers these days, but she had no intention at this late date of changing a system that had worked for generations.

She lay the puppy down beside its mother. It latched onto a teat and began sucking greedily. With a pang, she realized she had been hoping for a brown boy like his father. Perhaps it was just as well. If he had been a miniature McCreery, she might have been tempted to keep him. Still, she had a good feeling about this fellow. First-borns often have a special something that makes them come alive in the show ring, and the way he thrust his little legs out at the world made her think he would grow up to be a lot like his father. Tears threatened to overwhelm her again, and she wished for the thousandth time that McCreery were there beside her.

She shivered, suddenly chilled, and not only by regret.

A gust of cold air slipping under the door reminded her how dangerous it could be for the puppies if she let her mind wander. She had rigged up a heat lamp to keep the newborns warm; perhaps it wasn't enough. Puppies can survive awhile without food, but their biggest danger is the cold. They can't regulate their own temperatures. That's why she had pushed the ancient heater up as high as it would go. She grabbed a chunk of newspaper and rolled it into an impromptu draft catcher to slide under the door, but before she could lay it down, the door swung open with a bone-numbing blast of arctic air. A tall figure hurried inside, collar raised, a black-and-red checkered cap pulled down over his ears. Only his eyes, dark like her own, were visible.

"Oh, it's you," she said. "I thought you'd be supervising Mona's prime rib. How did you know I was here?"

"It was obvious," David answered, stomping snow off his boots.

"Was it?" She wondered why. "The puppies have started coming. They don't know it's Christmas." She glanced up at the window where the snow was piling up along the sill. "Good thing Susie waited to come inside to start delivering."

The room fell silent, as if she had said the wrong thing.

He folded his scarf, placed it carefully on the counter, and breathed a heavy sigh. She wondered if he was remembering another Christmas whelping thirty years earlier. Even a new Flying Ace bicycle with a silver horn under the tree didn't make up for her not being there when he woke up. Mona did her best to console him, but he wanted his mother. She thought back then that he would never forgive her. She still believed it today.

He peered over her shoulders, keeping his hands tucked in his pockets. Only Bess was allowed to touch a newborn. "You're sure the puppies are McCreery's?"

"Of course I'm sure," she snapped. The question of paternity was as important for show dogs as the royal family. "Hannah and I supervised the whole thing. In a way, I'm glad now that McCreery ..." She broke off unable to continue.

David stretched out a comforting hand, but she pulled back, unable to cope. She had almost resigned herself that McCreery would be lost forever — like the whippet that disappeared from Kennedy Airport after being shown at Westminster, or the puppies of a champion bulldog stolen from their own living room. A van with a dented right fender wasn't much of a clue, and it was the only one they had. The tattoo inside McCreery's ear would prevent him from being sold to a reputable breeder, but the thief probably wanted him for stud to pass off the puppies as some other dog's get.

She cleared the lump from her throat and attempted a triumphant smile. "Twelve weeks and the whole kit and caboodle will be Hannah's to deal with."

She turned her attention back to Susie. Another puppy arrived head first, curled in the fetal position. Bess weighed and measured her and then helped her to a teat beside her brother.

David smiled down at the scene. "It beats me how a first-time mother instinctively knows what to do. It's like Susie's done this a hundred times."

"Dogs are different from people," she observed wryly. If she hadn't been so preoccupied, she might have noticed the little catch in her son's voice.

Puppies sometimes arrive in pairs, and a third puppy, another black boy, was already on his way. She scooped up the first two and laid them down in a small cardboard box. A heating pad underneath a layer of soft towels would help keep them warm.

David waited until she sat back, then he reached inside

his coat pocket. A frown deepened on his face. Slowly, he unwrapped the newspaper and held its contents out like a gift. "I'm sorry, Mother."

She was silent for a long moment. She always said there is no such thing as a dog without flaws, but her gut told her this brown boy would have been almost perfect. Maybe it was because he looked so much like McCreery the day he was born. She stroked its little head with one finger. "He must have slipped out when Susie was playing in the snow. I had to call her in twice."

David's face looked like he had knocked the angel off the top of the Christmas tree. "What was I thinking, bringing a dead puppy here? Forgive me."

She waved a hand dismissively and turned back to Susie. Another puppy was on its way, and it was alive.

He rewrapped the tiny body in its newspaper shroud and laid it on the counter.

Before the morning was over, five healthy puppies — two black boys and three girls, two blacks and a brown — were lying together in a heap. Their eyes and ears were closed, but their noses worked fine, so they had no trouble searching out each other and their mother. Bess gave Susie a final pat on the head and struggled to her feet, joints cracking from sitting too long in one spot.

"All done then?"

She flinched. She had almost forgotten her son was there sitting quietly on a rusty folding chair. Her mind had been on the ice puppy. "A brown boy. So like his father," she whispered.

David hesitated, like a man braving the first swim after a long, cold winter. "You're entitled to pick of the litter as the stud fee, and now Hannah owes you for the whelping, too. You could keep one or even two — maybe a boy and a girl."

Her face tightened. "Hold it right there," she snapped.

"But without McCreery ..." He couldn't finish the thought.

She stuck her hand out like a shield. "No puppies!"

Defeated, he rose to leave.

She cupped an ear. "Wait! Did you hear something?"

He shook his head.

Bess got to her feet. "There it is again."

Susie peered over the side of the whelping pen, sniffing anxiously.

"Maybe," he said, humoring her.

Bess walked to the counter. Hands trembling, she unrolled the newspaper again. Frosty air rose off the tiny body inside, but the little chest was moving up and down. The puppy was breathing. Alive!

David's jaw dropped. "Hypothermia. The newspaper's saved him so far, but we've got to get more warmth into him."

She nodded. Her fingers were cold and tingled after holding the puppy only a few seconds. She glanced around the room for a solution. There was only one. She opened her flannel shirt and tucked the icy body inside.

"Should I call the vet?" he asked.

For answer, she slumped down on the floor, her back resting against the whelping box. The shallow rise and fall of the puppy's chest fell into rhythm with hers, taking in heat from her body, giving off cold from his. Peering down the neck of her shirt, she studied the sleeping puppy, so like the others that had come before him, yet different. Automatically, she rubbed her forefinger tenderly across the crown of his head.

David studied the scene with a gentle smile. "What will you name him?"

Her dark eyes flashed. "Hannah's. I'll call him Hannah's because that's whose puppy he is."

The hope on his face faded like ink on an old letter.

"You can't," he insisted, his voice too loud for the small room. "You need him, and he obviously needs you."

She waited a long minute before answering, gathering the strength to say what she must. "What I need is to be left alone. Go, your Christmas dinner's getting cold." She pulled her shirt collar up higher around her neck and closed her eyes.

The door clicked shut behind him.

She must have fallen asleep because when she awoke, she could feel no difference between her body temperature and the puppy's. He gawped and patted the air blindly, as though feeling for her. The gesture was familiar, like his father's. She leaned and breathed the warm puppy smell deep into her lungs. If he turned out to be half the dog his father was, there was no telling how far he could go. "You're going to be something special. Maybe even *the* one," she whispered.

Turning his head in the direction of her voice, the puppy opened its soft pink mouth and exhaled a long, contented yawn.

She yanked her hand back like she had seared it on a hot iron. She placed the puppy down beside Susie and watched him toddle his way blindly to his dinner. Using the edge of the whelping pen to push herself up, she rose and walked stiffly to the wall phone. She needed to do it now, or she might never find the courage. She studied the number she had written in pencil on the wall and dialed.

"Hannah?" she said when the voice on the other end answered. "The puppies have come. Three girls and three boys. No, I haven't changed my mind. Yes, all of them."

Chapter 8

Benny was the most miserable boy in Fairfield County. It wasn't his mother's weekend, he hadn't seen his friend Steffie all week, and Sonya had taken away his game player just because he forgot to empty the dishwasher. He walked barefoot over to his desk where a pile of homework worksheets were waiting and pushed them to one side. Life was bad enough without memorizing a bunch of kings that died before he was born. Besides, his eyes had been kind of itchy ever since Language Arts this morning. He pressed his nose against the mirror over his dresser and pulled down his eyelid. The skin, or whatever it was underneath his lid, looked red and squishy, and he decided he'd better show Dr. Kate on Monday. All that schoolwork could be damaging his eyes.

He went to the window and stared in the direction of the old woman's house. He hadn't talked to her for a couple of months, not since the night he met McCreery, but he had watched her from a distance. Odd as it seemed, his happiest time of day was spying on that decrepit old woman in her decrepit old house. At least then he knew for sure one person in the world was worse off than him.

What was that? He cupped a hand to an ear. Maybe it was only the March wind playing tricks. He threw open the window and listened again. Puppies! This time he was sure.

He hurried downstairs, climbed over the stone wall fence, and arrived in Bess's backyard. Dropping down on all fours, he crab-crawled behind a picnic table someone had left out all winter. The clouds had cleared, and the afternoon sun felt warm on his back. A portable pen was set up on the lee side of the house, and Susie hopped out. Five squealing puppies clawed at the sides and cried after her. The sixth, a round-bellied brown fellow, stared at him intently and wagged his bobbed tail. The puppy was too cute for a poodle, but he had seen all those trophies McCreery had won, and the puppy looked just like him. They both had curly brown coats and the amber eyes of the stuffed dog that used to sleep on his bed before his parents' divorce. When he squeezed its stomach, a music box inside played a lullaby.

The excitement of a new visitor was too much for the puppy, and the same eagerness for life that had turned him into a popsicle the day he was born grabbed hold of him again. He skittered back to the farthest corner of the pen and made a running leap. He just missed clearing the top and seesawed back and forth on the rim, legs running in air. He heaved himself off and fell back into the pen, rolling onto his back. Unfazed, he shook his coat and leaped again. This time he landed in a heap on the ground outside. His eyes widened in delighted surprise. A shiny-coated black boy who was nearly his twin started to follow but thought better of it.

Benny started to laugh but choked it back and scooted under the picnic table when a door creaked open. Bess stepped out of the house with a stack of magazines in her arms. The puppy scrambled toward her with a cheerful grin, unconcerned that he had escaped without parole. She gasped, and it seemed to Benny that a lifetime of feelings rose up in her lungs, threatening to suffocate her. She dropped the magazines on the picnic table and scooped up the puppy, holding him out with both hands to ward off the warm puppy smell.

She lowered the puppy back into the pen, picked up her magazines, and nearly stumbled over the foot sticking out from under the picnic table. She dropped her gaze, and Benny stared back at her. Balancing her magazines on one arm, she wriggled an index finger to summon him out.

Benny turned his head from side to side, hoping she was signaling some other boy.

"Yes, you," she called in a croaky voice. "Who else could I mean?"

He scrambled out and brushed off his knees, smiling sheepishly. "I dropped by to say hello to McCreery. I didn't want him to think I'd forgotten him."

Her eyes widened. Apparently, the boy hadn't seen any of the signs posted all over town. "He's not here," she said, voice cracking. She looked again at the boy, staring at the puppy with hungry eyes. "Say, how about I hire you to play with the puppies? They need someone to run them around and get them used to people. It'd just be until they go to Hannah's — six more weeks."

He turned to find six eager faces and twelve oversized paws scrabbling at the side of the pen, begging for attention. "No, thanks. I told you before. I'm not interested in poodles."

Her thick eyebrows flicked in surprise. "Most kids your age would give their eye teeth for an invitation like that." She shifted her magazines to her other arm. "If you don't want to help with the puppies, maybe you'd like to carry some of these magazines?"

"No, thanks," he said again. "My stepmother says I'm lazy." He made it sound like a virtue.

She stifled a chortle and handed him half her magazines. A couple of *Dog World* issues slithered off. The dates went back a couple of decades.

He bent to retrieve them. "You know, this job'd go a lot faster with a wheelbarrow."

"Wish we had one," she said, not sounding sorry at all. "Mona said if I was serious about retiring, I'd get them out of the living room. She's my twin sister."

He slapped his thigh. "So there are two of you. I never knew old people could be twins before."

She laughed her croupy laugh. It sounded rusty, like she hadn't used it in a while. "We've been twins for seven decades now. We're nothing alike, though."

Susie finished her business and came running. She gave Benny a friendly sniff and rubbed her muzzle against Bess's pant leg. Bess ruffled the dog's topknot and signaled Benny to follow her inside the puppy shed. Dozens of magazines, all with champion dogs on their covers, filled the counter. She dropped hers on top and nodded at the pile. "Drop yours there, too."

They landed with a thud. He bent over and rested his hands on his knees. "I'm not sure I should be doing all this heavy lifting. I'd hate to have to spend the night in the hot tub and skip my homework." He cleared a spot on the counter and hoisted himself up. "You got any kids?" he asked after a pause. As long as he kept her talking, she couldn't make him haul more magazines.

She plucked a dead leaf from a geranium that had managed to survive the winter and twirled it nervously between her thumb and forefinger. "David's a grown man. Thirty-five, no six. He lives over there." She pointed vaguely in the direction of the stone wall that divided the school from the dregs of Umpawaug Kennels.

"I've seen his cottage from Dr. Kate's office window, but I haven't had time to introduce myself. Keeping my room clean and stuff. You know."

"David and I aren't on the best of terms," she said and blushed, puzzled by her own honesty.

"What'd he do? Steal money out of your wallet?"

"Nothing like that. He thinks he knows what's best for me."

"Maybe you should listen."

She tossed the dead leaf away. "Too late."

Susie caught the sorrow in Bess's voice and leaned against her thigh. Susie might belong to Hannah now, but she was Umpawaug through and through. Bess laced her fingers through Susie's coat the way a drowning sailor clings to the gunwales of a lifeboat.

The blare of a horn made them both jump. Benny popped up like his seat was on fire. "My mom!"

She watched him scurry down the hill, arms windmilling. He reminded her of someone. She couldn't think who it was. It gave her an empty feeling inside, like an unfulfilled promise. In the distance, she could just make out the mail truck hurrying down Gallows Hill Road.

He must have seen it, too. He hung his head and walked slump-shouldered toward his dad's.

She raised herself off the bench and continued her work alone.

Chapter 9

Benny stuck his hands in his pockets and swaggered out of Dr. Kate's office, chin tucked, chest out. She had just appointed him official school messenger, which meant he was responsible for bringing the attendance sheet to the office every day. The job gave him the perfect excuse to stretch his legs and keep an eye on what was going on at the school.

Voices were coming from the playground where Steffie's class was having recess, and he decided the attendance sheet could wait. He readjusted his waistband and ambled over to where a bunch of kids were shooting hoops. Other kids were hanging out together in small groups. Sitting cross-legged on the porch, off by herself, was Steffie. At least, he thought it was Steffie. The girl's hair was tied up in braids on top of her head, and where her coat was open, he could see a dress with a bunch of little red and yellow flowers and a frilly white apron like a girl in a movie who loved Swiss cheese and goats. He thought she had painted freckles on her nose and cheeks, but he couldn't be sure. She was holding a thick book. Like he guessed, it was the *Diagnostic and Statistical Manual.*

Steffie pushed the bangs out of her eyes and looked up. "I'm studying up on Asperger's. There's plenty of good stuff in here that tells me all about my symptoms. I'm thinking about making a list and posting it on the refrigerator."

He gave her a doubtful look. "You're kidding, right?"

"My mother doesn't think so. For example, I shouldn't be talking to you. Asperger's kids don't know how to make friends, remember?"

He tossed the attendance sheet onto the porch and plunked himself down beside her. "Maybe I can help. I've got lots of friends." He blushed. "Well, maybe not so many, but there's Adam. He's got Asperger's, too."

"Friends suck. As soon as I make one, my mother yanks me out of school. She'll do it again. Wait and see." She wrinkled her nose and made her freckles pucker.

He decided she had used a brown magic marker. He nodded at her thick leather boots like mountain climbers wear. "You into goats or something?"

She stared at him for a second and her face cracked into a smile. "I never met a goat I didn't like," she said.

His hands tighten into fists. Was she mocking him?

She held up a hand and waved her words away. "Sorry, it's a joke. I never met a goat in my life. You?"

He shook his head with an embarrassed grin. "Funny. Personally, I like dogs. Except for poodles. I'm into real dogs." He bent his head closer and looked hard. "Say, are you supposed to be staring at me like that? I thought you said Aspies don't make eye contact."

She brushed at her skirt and grinned. "Good one. Not much gets past you, does it?"

His chest swelled with pride. His heart soared. Maybe Steffie wouldn't turn out to be just another girl who thought he was a couple of nickels short of a quarter.

His stomach gave a loud rumble, and he remembered the cookies the school secretary kept in her desk drawer. He gave Steffie a sharp salute, ironed the attendance sheet with his hand, and headed for the office.

He had only been back in class a few minutes when

boredom began creeping in again. Mrs. Santos was teaching about gerunds and participles and a lot of stuff that was a complete waste of time. He had been speaking English for years and nobody had ever complained they couldn't understand him. He was thinking about having a little nap when he spotted something suspicious out the classroom window. A stranger in a tweed jacket and a red-and-black checkered cap was peering under the deck of the main building the way spies did on TV when they were hunting for secret messages.

"Gotta go, Mrs. Santos," he called, holding his crotch and jiggling up and down like he couldn't hold it. He dashed out the door without bothering to hide the fact that he was heading in the opposite direction from the bathroom. At least he had the presence of mind to grab Volume A of the *Encyclopedia Britannica* in case he needed a weapon. Volume A was one of the thickest and the only one he'd had a chance to look at so far. Not to mention it was closest to the door. Mrs. Santos probably thought he was planning to read it on the pot.

Fortunately, the stranger was so engrossed in looking behind the bushes he didn't notice Benny sneaking up behind. "Stay where you are," he commanded. He had been planning for his words to come out in a deep voice, but they eked out in a squeak.

The stranger spun around. Even under his tweed jacket, the strength in his muscles showed. "Aren't you supposed to be in class?" he asked, like Benny was the one doing something wrong.

Benny wished he had let someone know where he was heading. Think of the irony — a word he had learned from Mrs. Santos one time when he had been paying attention. A few minutes earlier he thought nothing exciting would ever happen to him, and now here he was in terrible danger, maybe about to die. "If you know what's good for you, you'll beat it out of here. Dr. Kate's probably calling the cops this minute."

"You don't say," said the stranger, apparently unconcerned.

Benny considered telling him he had been duck hunting with his dad before and was a good shot with a rifle, but he decided to memorize the man's face instead so he could give the cops a good description in case he was wanted for anything big. The stranger had a shadow around his mouth and chin where he hadn't shaved, and his thick eyebrows reminded him of someone. He couldn't remember who. The stranger reached into his pocket, and Benny was sure he was a goner, but the man only pulled out a pipe. He tapped it on the bottom of his shoe before sticking it unlit in his mouth. "I'm David, David Rutledge," he said.

Benny felt a rush of relief. "Any relation to Bess Rutledge?"

David's eyes widened. "She's my mother. You know her?"

Benny shrugged. "Sure. She's a real nut about dogs, at least poodles."

David laughed. "That's her. At least, she used to be. Actually, I'm kind of worried about her."

Benny tipped his head. "Really? She seemed fine to me except old."

David picked up a stick and broke it into little pieces. "You know what depression is?"

"Sure. Plenty of kids at my school have it. Not me, though. I wouldn't be caught dead."

David covered a laugh with a cough. He scattered the broken sticks on the ground and studied them as though they could tell the future. "My mother's dreamed of winning Westminster her whole life. She's been invited dozens of times, but something always seems to get in the way."

"Weird!"

Benny picked up a stick of his own. "You married?"

David shook his head. "Divorced, no kids."

Benny nodded knowledgably. "My mom's divorced. My dad, too, but he's married again. Maybe you should meet Dr. Kate. She's not bad looking for a meeting doctor." He pointed to a second floor window overhead. "That's her office up there."

David gave a hard look as though hoping for something. "A meeting doctor? What does a meeting doctor do exactly?"

Benny shrugged. "Nothing, just have meetings with kids all day. Parents have to pay her lots of money, and all she does is sit around and talk about feelings. I'm thinking about being one myself."

David stuck his unlit pipe in his mouth to stifle a laugh. "Sounds like a good deal."

Benny nodded. "Dr. Kate would probably like to meet you. She loves taking people around our school." He lowered his voice conspiratorially. "I think she's trying to get money to keep the school open." He gave David a piercing look. "Say, do you have a job?"

"Not as good as a meeting doctor. I'm what they call a CPA — certified public accountant. I help people manage their money."

"You have to know your times tables?"

"I'm afraid so."

"That's what I thought. Sounds boring." He broke the stick he had been holding into tiny pieces and threw them on the ground. When they didn't tell him anything special, he asked something he'd been wondering about. "What's so great about this Westminster, anyway?"

David tugged on the beak of his cap. "Sorry, I was brought up believing everyone knows Westminster. Actually, it's the most famous dog show in America, maybe the world. Twenty-five hundred dogs, two hundred sixty-five breeds.

It's the oldest continuous sporting event in America except for the Kentucky Derby. They've held it every year since 1877, through blizzards, national depressions, and two world wars."

Benny thought he would probably go if someone gave him a ticket but watching a bunch of fancy dogs parading around a ring wasn't his idea of fun. His eyes lit up. "Say, I've got a great idea. If Bess doesn't like the puppy, why doesn't she enter McCreery? He's a great-looking dog. He could win Westminster for sure."

David's eyes narrowed. "You know McCreery?"

"Sure. I'm Benny Neusner. McCreery's practically my best friend."

David took off his cap and rubbed his hand across his head before replacing it. "McCreery's gone. Stolen. That's why I'm here. Someone said they thought they'd seen him at the school."

Benny gasped. "I saw Bess yesterday and she didn't say a thing. We've got to find him." He turned and headed for the street.

"Wait!" David called. "You can't just leave school without permission. McCreery was stolen weeks ago."

Benny flung out his arms. "We've got to do something."

"Believe me, I've tried, but we can't give up hope. He still might be found."

Benny spat. He knew all about hope. It led to broken hearts.

David looked as though he understood, but what he said was, "For my mother's sake, I have to keep trying."

Mothers were something Benny knew about. He looked up at the sky, his hands steepled together as if praying. "I'll find you, McCreery. That's a promise."

David frowned. "You can't make a promise like that," he stammered.

Benny shrugged. “I just did.”

“I don’t want you to get hurt,” David said, his voice softer.

“No sweat. I’m going to find him.”

Chapter 10

David watched Benny disappear inside and turned to leave. He was startled to find a slight woman about his own age blocking his path. Her eyebrows were pulled into a slight frown, and he wondered how long she had been eavesdropping on his conversation with Benny. He thought she had chosen her navy blue suit so people would take her seriously, but her sling-back heels with crisscrossed straps revealed a lighter side. "Dr. Kate, I presume," he said, tipping his cap with an exaggerated old-fashioned bow.

She held back a smile, recognizing the literary allusion. "You presume correctly. You have an appointment?" she asked, suspicion clouding her tone.

"I was looking for my mother's dog, and Benny and I got to talking. He's been telling me about you. I was curious." Her frown deepened, and he added quickly, "Oops, that didn't come out right. What I meant was I've been meaning to introduce myself. I'm your neighbor, David Rutledge."

She hesitated, then held out her hand. "Kate Kumar. You're the man who lives in the cottage behind us?"

He wondered how she guessed. "That's me," he admitted, holding her hand a moment longer than necessary. He checked her fingers. No rings but a gold bracelet dangled off one wrist. A little dirt shown beneath her clear nail polish. He had noticed her earlier with some children in the garden. Maybe Benny was right. She might be worth taking a chance on. She was intelligent and kind, at least to children like Benny, not to mention beautiful with her café au lait skin and surprising green eyes.

She tucked her hand behind her back, blushing. "I was helping the children plant zinnias. I hadn't planned to get involved. It just happened."

Something in her manner made him think she wasn't spontaneous very often. "Sounds like fun."

Her ankle turned in for no apparent reason, and she teetered a little. The movement was so slight he almost missed it. It must be an effort to chase after a bunch of kids like Benny all day in heels.

"A lot of the neighbors weren't too happy when they heard we were opening a therapeutic school. People aren't always comfortable about special kids, especially one with problems."

He smiled. "Most people probably think your school's an improvement over a bunch of barking dogs."

The tension around her mouth eased. "I hope I didn't insult you, but I can't have strangers hanging around my students. Benny spends too much time wandering the campus when he's supposed to be in class. Fortunately, I can keep an eye on him from my office window."

He wondered whether she had ever watched for him. She had known where his cottage was. "Benny seems like a good kid but maybe not too sure of himself."

She looked down, the tension reappearing in her shoulders. "I don't want to be rude, but I can't talk about my students."

He stepped back, waving a hand and smiling. "I didn't mean to pry. I'm sure your job is challenging."

She pushed back her bangs, revealing a smooth, broad forehead, but the dark circles under her eyes told him she had been losing sleep over something. "Some special children can have a brilliant understanding of a complicated emotion one minute and throw a pencil against the wall the next because they can't solve a simple math problem like two-times-three. It can be confusing."

He lowered his eyes. "I hope I haven't added to your difficulties. I had to give Benny some bad news"

Her face fell. "Oh?"

"A dog of my mother's was stolen. Apparently, Benny was fond of him."

"How terrible. Your mother must be devastated."

The thoughtful look on her face reminded him she was a shrink. Some men might feel intimated, but he was intrigued. "That's putting it mildly. She still has a whole litter of puppies — one that's extremely promising — but she's refused to keep any of them. I suspect she's afraid she'll get her heart broken."

All she did was nod, but somehow he felt she knew something about broken hearts. "Actually, Benny's given me an idea," he said.

She tipped her chin, interested. "Really?"

"I've taken on the puppy myself, hoping to get my mother back in the game. I thought Benny might like to help me, maybe even enter the puppy in a couple of dog shows. Just small ones, nothing big."

"Why Benny? He owns a pet gerbil and a couple of garter snakes, but no dog."

He leaned forward. He wanted to please her more than anyone else in a very long time. "It might help him get over McCreery."

She drew herself upright. "Help? Or lead to more heartbreak? Not to mention Benny's father would never allow it."

"Lots of kids get over losing one dog by getting another."

Her jaw tightened. "Benny's a student in this school for

a reason. No offense, but better leave him in the hands of the professionals."

One side of his mouth slid into a half-smile. "It's just a puppy, not rocket science."

"I'm talking about his heart, not his brain," she shot back. "Your intentions may be good, but Benny's had enough disappointments in his life already. I can't let you build up his hopes for nothing." She looked at her watch. "If there's nothing else?"

He pulled down the beak of his cap, camouflaging his face. "No, nothing." He banged the gate behind him, wondering how Benny ever thought Dr. Kumar could be his type.

⚜⚜⚜

"Benny's been off his game lately, have you noticed?" Benny's dad asked his wife, Sonya.

"Noticed? I'll say. I left a tray of chocolate chip cookies cooling on the counter when I went to change my shoes, and when I got back, he hadn't snitched a single one. You could have knocked me over with a feather."

"Think he's worried about something?"

"Could be he's still pining over that dog he wants. I wouldn't worry. Kids are always upset about something."

"Maybe, but he'll never get into law school with his grades."

"Law school? He hasn't even made it to high school yet. Remember what Dr. Kate said: Benny's not you."

"Shrinks don't know everything. Benny's just like me. I needed someone to keep my nose to the grindstone when I was his age. Now it's my turn."

CHAPTER 11

Funhouse Friday was a special time for students to relax with their friends, provided they finished their class work, did their homework, and stayed in charge all week. Benny usually had some make-up work to do first, but not today, mostly because it was standardized testing week and homework was cancelled. Hands in his pockets, he sauntered around the converted carriage house hoping to find Steffie. He didn't see her right away, but he did notice his friend Adam Sarkejian. Adam was thirteen and already doing calculus, but he was shy and didn't hang out much. Mostly he was crazy about Prince Valiant, his favorite cartoon character, and drew him every chance he got. His greatest regret was he was born too late to meet Hal Foster, the man who created Prince Valiant, but at least he got to pass by the house where Hal used to live every day on his way to school.

For once Adam didn't have a colored pencil in his hand. He was playing chess with a girl Benny didn't recognize. That was a surprise. The only new student this semester was Steffie, and this girl looked nothing like her. No British boarding school uniform; no Swiss goatherd outfit. This girl's hair was blond and hung down in corkscrew curls. Red ribbons were tied at the top of every one. It must have taken hours to fix. Her frilly white blouse had a matching red bow at the neck and topped a short red skirt with white polka dots. Black patent leather shoes and white socks with lace rims finished off her outfit. He had never seen anyone look so out of it except some goofball little kid who sang about lollipops in a black-and-white movie. Not exactly girlfriend material.

Benny sat at the far end of the long table and pulled his geography book out of his backpack. He had chosen it because it was the thickest. He didn't want the girl to think he was a dummy or anything. He gave the chess players another look over the top of the page, and that's when he realized his mistake. The girl *was* Steffie and from what he could tell from her body language, she wasn't enjoying herself. She stood and arched her back like a cat.

"I'm tired of sitting," she announced to the room. "The List says Aspies can concentrate for long periods of time, but so what?" She nodded at a small girl reading a book by herself. Even though the day was warm, the girl was huddled inside a wooly white coat that looked like polar bear fur. "Taylor will finish my game."

Silently, Taylor stuck a finger between the pages to mark her place and joined Adam at the table. Neither of them said a word while she studied the board. She chose a pawn and made her move.

Steffie picked a chair opposite Benny and helped herself to popcorn. He was glad she had decided to give up the chess game. He didn't want her to find out he couldn't remember all those crazy moves. Besides, this was as good a time as any to tell her about McCreery, but her eyes were focused on something over his shoulder. He turned. Dr. Kate was opening the carriage house door for a man he recognized. She had a smile on her face like she had just won the lottery.

"Is that man Dr. Kate's husband?" Steffie asked, twirling a corkscrew curl around her index finger.

"Naw, he's my friend David. She's not married. All she does is work. I'm trying to help her with that."

"You must be getting through. She's really putting the moves on him."

"Dr. Kate always looks like that when she's trying to get money for the school. To tell the truth, the first time they met, things didn't go so great. He thought she was a control freak, and she said he was sticking his nose in where it didn't belong. I've been working on it. I told her David is crazy about the school, and I convinced him she'd love to show him around." He hooked his thumbs under his armpits and grinned. He was convinced the new blue rubber bands on his braces made him look cool.

Steffie jutted out her head like a turtle. "Jeez, don't you think they're kind of old for dating?"

He looked again. David's smile was as big as Dr. Kate's. If he didn't know better, he'd think they were flirting. "Dr. Kate says you're never too old, but she might have been trying to convince me I have plenty of time for sex." He clapped his hand over his mouth. Too late, he realized he shouldn't mention the "s" word to a girl with a head full of ribbons. "Sorry, I've got a lot on my mind."

"Can I help?"

He shrugged, his happy mood sliding away like custard on a fork. "Someone stole McCreery. He's my best friend — for a dog," he added tactfully. "He's been gone for weeks. I'm afraid if we don't find him soon ..." His voice trailed off, unable to finish. He wanted to find McCreery so badly he even dreamed about it. In fact, he'd had the same dream practically every night since he learned McCreery was missing. Dr. Kate warned him that dreams are about our wishes and don't always come true, but he was sure this dream was real.

She reached out her hand, and he thought she might touch his arm. "I'm really sorry," she said instead. "There must be something we can do." She fussed with the lace tatting around the rim of her sock and then tilted her head up. "I've got it. We can make posters and spread them around town in the limo after school."

He dropped his chin. David had already tried that, but she was being awfully nice. She had never even met McCreery, and Aspies aren't supposed to be that interested in other people's problems. "It won't hurt to try. We can't give up."

She smiled. "True. Now, we need a description."

He straightened his shoulders. "That's easy. McCreery's the world's most famous poodle, but he doesn't look like one. You should see all the trophies he's won."

She nodded. "That's probably why he was stolen." She rose and grabbed her backpack from the back of her chair. "Come on. You tell me what to say and I'll type."

He scooped a last handful of popcorn and followed her to the art supply shelf. They had to find McCreery soon. They just had to.

Chapter 12

Benny shivered at the end of the school driveway with his hands stuffed in his pockets. Steffie had helped him tack up posters near every school in Fairfield County, and the cold weather hadn't bothered him a bit. Now, waiting for his mother, the sharp March wind cut through to his bones. He would have punched anybody in the face who said they felt sorry for him. That wasn't exactly what he had done to get kicked out of his old school, but a girl said the wrong thing at the right time, and her desk sort of got knocked over. The principal told his dad it was one meltdown too many, and he would have to go. No one figured out he actually had a crush on the girl.

He stepped out into the middle of the road and peered ahead as far as he could see. No car yet, but at least his mother was coming. Not like last weekend when she had a really good excuse. A sales clerk at the mall had insisted on checking her credit card and made her so late getting started they wouldn't have gotten home in time to find out whether the lady on TV would win all that money — something she and Benny were both really excited about. Saturday there was always too much traffic, and besides, they would just have to turn around and face more cars on Sunday.

He pushed up his sleeve and checked his watch.

Realizing how long he had been standing in the cold made him notice how tired his legs were of holding him up. It was the new gym teacher's fault. He was on a kick that everyone should pass President Clinton's physical fitness program. Personally, he didn't see how it would help America if every kid his age could do a bunch of squats. Maybe it would come in handy in countries where people ate dinner sitting on rugs and had to get up and down a lot, but personally, he preferred a table and chair.

If he had known his mother would be this late, he could have spent a little extra time hunting for McCreery. He had a regular routine he followed every day. Each afternoon on his way home from school, he checked under all the trees and bushes by the side of the road. Every night, he snuck food from the kitchen and left it in a bowl where McCreery could find it. Sometimes, he could only manage a leftover broccoli casserole or Tofu Lemongrass Surprise, but he figured it was better than nothing. He was even planning to take a morning off from school soon to check out Gallows Hill, so-called because a British spy had gotten himself hanged there during the American Revolution. He didn't believe in ghosts or anything, but McCreery was too smart to hang out in a place like that after dark.

He knew for sure McCreery was on his way home. The dream he'd had every night was proof. A fat man with pointy teeth and a scar like lightning was holding McCreery prisoner in a cave somewhere. He'd kidnapped McCreery because he was the most famous stud dog in the world, and he wanted his puppies so he could sell them for a ton of money. The man kept McCreery locked in a cage with a lot of bars, only when he opened the door so McCreery and the lady dog could do their thing, McCreery bit the man's rear and ran. He ran so fast he made it back to Redding in practically no time. By then, he was hungry and tired and his poor paws were bloody and sore from all that running.

He lay down in some leaves under a tree and fell asleep, and that was the part where Benny always woke up sobbing because right now, McCreery was out there waiting for him to bring him home. The colors in his dream were getting brighter all the time, so he knew McCreery would be home soon. Maybe even tonight.

The cough and sputter of his mother's battered old Chevy reached Benny's ears. He dashed down the stairs and slid into the passenger seat.

She blew him an air kiss and began rummaging in her purse. She held up her prize lipstick and craned her neck toward the rearview mirror. "It's only the Golden Arches tonight, Benny. I've had a lot of expenses this month," she said.

He turned his jacket pocket inside out. Crisp dollar bills fell onto the seat. "Surprise!"

She pulled her half-painted mouth down in fake disapproval. "Benny Neusner," she sing-songed. "Have you been 'borrowing' money off your father's dresser again?"

He hung his head. "Gee, Mom. He doesn't even miss it."

She slapped his thigh playfully and giggled. "You bad boy."

He laughed, too, a bit nervously. "You're not mad?"

She flipped her fine, straight hair over her shoulder. "Honey, that money's as much mine as Sonya's. If it was up to her, you'd be living in poverty like me. No nice clothes, no fancy restaurants. I lost my child support the minute I let you live with your dad, but I gladly made the sacrifice so you could live in that huge mansion." She waved up the hill at the handsome brick house and sighed.

Benny winced guiltily. "But Sonya says ..."

She cut him off. "Are you going to listen to that woman or your own mother? You don't see Sonya eating at the Golden Arches, do you?"

Benny didn't think the Golden Arches sounded so bad. He remembered the garlic spinach and cold boiled eggs Sonya had sent in his lunch box today. He had wanted to punch her one for saying he was getting fat like his mother. If they went to the Golden Arches, maybe he could sneak out a cheeseburger for McCreery. Dogs have a terrific sense of smell, and the aroma would tell him he was on the trail home — especially if it had lots of onions and extra cheese.

He beamed conspiratorially. "I'm practically starving for a double bacon cheeseburger. I've got enough for extra large fries and a drink, too."

Instead of the approval he expected, his mother exhaled a heart-piercing sigh. "Maybe someday I'll get to go to The Spinning Wheel. That's where your father takes Sonya. He loves the Caesar salad, the double-stuffed potatoes, those thick, juicy steaks."

Benny squirmed. He could hardly stand it when his mother was upset. "I'll take you."

She peeked at him, her smile encouraging. "How much you got?"

He told her.

She wrinkled her nose. "Too little."

His chin dropped like a popped balloon. He wished he had taken a bill or two from Sonya's purse, too. She deserved it, the way she lied about his mom.

They rode in silence for a couple of miles, past the old Burritt's Farm and Redding Elementary School. As they approached the intersection for Bethel, she perked up. "We've got enough for Buffy's Buffet," she said, veering left.

"Do they have double bacon cheeseburgers?" His dog book said all dogs love cheese, and McCreery deserved a big chunk after what he had been through.

She shook her head and started to giggle. "No, sweetie.

Buffy's is a real restaurant. All you can eat."

He rubbed his little paunch and hung his head. "You won't tell Sonya? I'm supposed to be watching my diet."

She took his hand and squeezed. "No way, darling. Eat your heart out."

CHAPTER 13

Benny's mom dropped him off at the end of the driveway and tooted the horn good-bye. Benny checked his pockets to be sure the treats for McCreery were safe — the crust off a macaroni and cheese casserole, two buffalo wings without the bones, a beef taco mostly in one piece, and a slice of apple pie — but he was so worried about what Sonya would say if she smelled pepperoni pizza on his breath that he was two-thirds up the hill before he remembered to check for McCreery. Tired as he was, he trudged back down the hill and started over. McCreery was close by; he was sure of it. He'd practically felt McCreery's breath on his face last night.

He stood back and took a hard look at the scene in front of him. He had studied it dozens of times before, but tonight something seemed different. He tipped his head way back, so he was staring straight up at his mother's star, when he noticed a pattern that seemed strangely familiar in the way the tops of the pine trees fit together. He half closed his eyes and squinted. Yes, it was the same pattern he had seen in his dream! McCreery was so close, he could practically smell him.

His heart started pounding, and all that oxygen getting to his brain must have been the reason he suddenly got a terrific idea. He had seen a program on late night television where the good guys were trying to find a chest with lots of gold and valuable stuff hidden in a cave. He couldn't remember where exactly, but the place had a bunch of coconuts. The hero did what they call a "triangulation," which isn't that hard. All you do is pick three spots, and that's where you'll find what you're looking for. It could work for McCreery.

He found the flashlight in his backpack and snapped it on. Taking the star as point one and the tops of the trees as point two, he moved his arm until the flashlight formed the third point of a triangle with the star and the trees. He hustled to the spot where the flashlight pointed. He pushed against a branch and looked. Nothing! How could that be?

His legs collapsed like wet spaghetti. The ground underneath him was cold, but he felt peaceful lying there in the quiet night. Even the birds were silent. He closed his eyes.

And then he heard it: the beckoning call of the dog he had dreamed of all his life, and this time it was real. He jumped to his feet and raced to a spot only a few yards away. He pointed his flashlight. The wobbling light illuminated a long ear, and then a shoulder, and then a bobbed tail that flicked once or twice before giving up the effort. An eyeball blinked back at him.

McCreery!

Benny dropped to his knees. Just like in the dream, McCreery's coat was shaggy and full of burs. Bloody sores caked his foot pads. His dull eyes were pleading for help.

Benny held out his hand. "Come on, boy, get up."

McCreery made a brave effort to rise, whimpered softly, and rolled over onto his side.

"Up, boy," Benny begged, snapping his fingers for encouragement. McCreery tried his best, feet running in air, but he was too weak to gain purchase.

What to do? McCreery couldn't lie there forever. Benny

reached under his belly and tried lifting him up on his feet, but McCreery jerked away with a sharp yelp. Now what? He remembered the dog book said a person could tell a sick dog by touching its nose. He stuck a finger out tentatively. Hot, crusty leather met his touch.

He needed to think. He wasn't sure he could cure a sick dog. Bess could help, but she was the last person he'd ask. If she had sold him McCreery when he asked, this never would have happened. He wouldn't have let McCreery out of his sight for a single minute. Besides, she would probably want him back.

He rose and gave McCreery a gentle pat on the head. "Stay, boy," he ordered, as if the poor dog was able to go anywhere. "I'll be right back."

He raced up the driveway, his lungs wheezing like a broken accordion, but he didn't care if the effort took his last breath. McCreery was meant to be his dog, and Fate was giving him another chance. Who cared if McCreery used to belong to Bess? She didn't deserve such a nice dog, a dog that looked up at him so trustingly with those sad eyes. He and McCreery were meant to be together. It was Destiny. Why else would his mother have dawdled a few extra minutes over that second piece of cherry cheesecake? If she had dropped him off at his dad's a few minutes earlier, McCreery might not have gotten there yet; a few minutes later, and he might have crawled on. Like the dog book said, dogs and humans sometimes have special powers of communication, and that's how it was with him and McCreery. They were a team, a boy and his dog forever. Just let his dad or anyone else try to come between them now.

He let himself in the back door and tiptoed upstairs. It was early for his dad and Sonya to be locked up in their bedroom, but that's where they were. For once, he was glad. He grabbed the dog book from where he kept it handy on top of the toilet and tiptoed back downstairs to the kitchen.

Flipping through the pages, he didn't find a lot of helpful information about a dog that wouldn't get up. Then he remembered his mother always gave him chicken soup when he was sick. He pulled a red-and-white can off the shelf and emptied it into a bowl. McCreery wouldn't care if it wasn't hot, and he didn't have time to waste. Cradling the bowl carefully in both hands, he hurried back down the hill.

He found McCreery lying on his side, panting. Benny held the bowl under McCreery's nose and moved it back and forth so the dog could get a good whiff. McCreery didn't move. Benny tried again to lift him to his feet, but McCreery flopped in his arms like an empty sack. Hot tears ran down Benny's cheeks. Even his dog book wasn't any help. He had run out of ideas. Then he remembered a favorite saying of his mother's: "Time heals all wounds." He would wait a little longer, and let time do the healing.

CHAPTER 14

Bess's arm throbbed from lying too long in one spot. She could change her position, but what was the point? Some other part would start to hurt instead. Besides, pain was a good thing. It kept her mind off the hurt inside.

Just to be contrary, she rolled over anyway. Her toes bumped against something at the foot of the bed, and her heart gave a little leap. "McCreery!" she breathed, and then she remembered. It was only the tray Mona had left for dinner, still untouched. Homemade chicken soup, to judge from the aroma, as if chicken soup could fix what ailed her.

A knock came and the door opened a crack. Bess lay still, imitating sleep. She hoped it wasn't David again trying to persuade her to keep the brown puppy. The puppies were almost old enough to leave for Hannah's, and her son was growing more insistent. The scent of hyacinths reached her, and she knew it was her sister.

Mona glanced at the untouched bowl on the tray. She sat on the side of the bed and yanked back the duvet, slopping some soup onto the bed. "This has got to stop," she insisted, shaking Bess's shoulder. "Sit up! I'm talking to you."

Bess rose up on one elbow as though roused from deep sleep. "What is it? What's happened?"

Mona jabbed Bess's sore arm, making her wince.

"Nothing's happened, and nothing's going to improve until you get another dog. McCreery's gone. There are six perfectly good puppies in the whelping shed. Pick one."

Bess hung her head. "I can't …"

"Don't start that 'I can't' business with me, young lady. You can and you will. Our doctor says we could live to be a hundred, and I don't intend to go on like this for another three decades."

Bess couldn't help a small smile. It was so like her sister to take her pain and transform it into a burden for herself. Still, in a way, Mona was right. They had been carrying each other's emotional baggage all their lives.

Mona rose, chest thrust out triumphantly. "That's better. Now, which one will it be? The brown boy? He looks the most like his father."

Bess rolled back onto her pillows, a small moan escaping. She didn't want a puppy that looked like McCreery. She wanted McCreery, but there was no getting past Mona this time. She would have to choose. Better make it one of the females. The brown girl with the charming smile was pet quality. That's what she wanted, wasn't it? A good companion dog?

Mona tapped her foot impatiently. "Well?"

Before Bess could answer, someone banged on the front door. Mona looked out the window. The gas lamps gave off enough light to see. She turned to her sister with a puzzled look. "It's that strange boy."

Bess bolted upright. "McCreery!" she breathed. This time she was certain. Her dog had come home to her.

McCreery must have recognized the sound of Bess's car because as soon as she opened the door, he struggled to his feet. He managed a soft "woof," and slipped back down on the ground, too weak to stand.

Benny rushed to McCreery's side and slid his hands underneath. Once again he tried lifting the big dog, but as before, McCreery whimpered and jerked away.

"Let me see," Bess said, pushing Benny aside. Tenderly, with expert movements, she felt along McCreery's spine and joints. She drew a deep breath. "Thank goodness. Nothing's broken."

"Maybe if we try lifting him together," Benny suggested. "You take one end, and I'll take the other."

She shook her head. "We might hurt him. Let him do it himself if he can."

Benny dropped down on his haunches and stuck out his hand. Bess stood beside him, her hand out, too. "Here, McCreery. Come, boy," they called.

The dog tried and failed and tried again. Benny and Bess held their breaths. McCreery made one last scramble and rose on tottering legs like a newborn colt.

"Don't feel bad if he comes to me," Benny said. "I'm the one who found him when everyone else gave up."

"Except me," Bess said, "but thank you."

"Here, boy."

"Here, McCreery."

The dog looked from one to the other. First Benny, then Bess.

"You can visit him every day if you want," Benny promised.

Bess said nothing and didn't move.

"He can still love you. I won't mind," Benny said, his voice growing louder, as if to make his words come true.

Slowly, slowly, the dog took a few steps forward. He turned his head toward Benny and gently licked his cheek.

"See, he picked me," Benny shouted one last time, and watched tearfully as McCreery slid his head under Bess's hand and closed his eyes.

Benny got to his feet and ran.

"You can have one of the puppies, any one you want," Bess called after him. Just as she expected, Benny kept running. She had been in Benny's shoes before. He would always want McCreery, no matter what. She supported McCreery onto the backseat of her car one end at a time and took him home.

Chapter 15

Kate had her hand on her office doorknob, ready to leave, when she heard the knock. She glanced at her watch and sighed. Clients didn't just drop in without an appointment. Who could it be at this late hour? She signaled Lotus, her white mixed-breed dog, back into her hidey hole and swung the door open. A short woman with curly gray hair stood before her with her arms crossed. Kate knew the gesture was defensive and not aggressive, as most people thought.

Kate smiled, hoping to ease the older woman's discomfort. "You're Bess Rutledge, aren't you? How can I help you?"

Bess stepped back. "I'm not here to get my head screwed on straight, if that's what you think. It's about Benny." She peered past Kate into the office, as if checking his whereabouts. "You know him, I believe."

Kate glanced at her watch. She was already late for the seminar she needed for her therapy license, but she waved Bess inside and pointed to one of the facing chairs. She knew it took courage for Bess to come, and she was curious. Still, professional ethics compelled her to say, "I can't discuss the children I work with."

Bess rubbed one hand over the other, as if applying an expensive lotion, and looked around the room. "I've never been in a mental health professional's office before."

"I'm glad you came," Kate said, surprised to find she meant it.

Beth took a deep breath, as if about to plunge off a high diving board. "I didn't know how to be a good mother to my son. I'm trying to do better with the boy."

Up until that minute, Kate's impression had been that David's mother was only interested in her dogs, yet here she was, worried about Benny. Kate decided to make up the seminar another time and leaned in closer.

"You may know Benny found a dog of mine that was stolen," Bess continued. She posed it as a half-question and didn't wait for an answer. "He was counting on keeping the dog for himself, but that's impossible. I'm afraid his heart is broken, and I was hoping you could help."

Kate started so speak, but Bess interrupted as if eager to get it all out.

"Benny thinks it was some kind of miracle he found McCreery — a sign they are meant to be together — but McCreery let him know he prefers to stay with me." She lowered her voice confidentially. "McCreery and I have been together since he was a puppy. I delivered him into the world with my own hands." Her voice choked. "He means everything to me, but that doesn't mean I want to break the boy's heart. I've done that enough in my life, and I want it to stop, believe me."

Kate met her gaze. "I do believe you."

Bess's shoulders relaxed. "I offered him one of McCreery's puppies, but he refused. I couldn't come up with a better idea, and then I thought of you." She stared pointedly at the diplomas lining the wall behind Kate's desk. "Maybe you can think of a way to fix it." She sat back in her chair and waited.

Now that it was Kate's turn to speak, she didn't know what to say. "I'm sorry" was all she could think of.

When it was obvious nothing more was forthcoming, Bess rose. "Well, if that's all ..."

Kate waved her back down with a weak hand. It fell onto her lap like a dropped fly ball. "I wish I could help, but there are some outcomes therapy can't change, and this is one of them. Benny will have to get over his hurt in the usual way: he will have to find another dog to love." She flinched, as she realized her words could apply to people, not just dogs, and to her own broken heart, not just Benny's. Fortunately, David's mother hadn't seemed to notice. Or had she?

Bess' eyes scanned the bookshelves, the Oriental rug, the spot on Kate's desk where family photos might have been. Finally, she looked directly at Kate and said, "I think my son David is growing fond of you."

Kate blinked in surprise. She didn't think David would discuss his feelings about her with his mother. Still, Benny had said more than once that David was just like him, always thinking of his mother first. Some men never grew out of it. That was a highway to disappointment she didn't want to travel.

Bess seemed to read her concern. "Of course, he hasn't said anything directly, but lately I've noticed a lot of 'Kate this' and 'Kate that.' My sister Mona pointed it out first. Now that I've met you, I see why. You and I are kind of alike."

Kate squirmed in her chair. She didn't enjoy people analyzing her. "We are?"

Bess laughed, as though pleased with herself. "My kennel, your school. The kind of women people think don't have real lives."

Kate felt something loosen inside and surprised herself by laughing, too. "You mean a man in her life?"

"Exactly!"

Smiling, both women stood at once. "Thank you for coming," Kate said.

Bess held out her hand, then jerked it back like she had touched a hot stove. "Is there a charge?"

Kate reddened. She spent all day talking to people she needed to keep at a professional distance. She had let herself hope for something different this time. "Not at all."

The tightness around Bess's mouth eased. "I wasn't sure. I wanted to do the right thing."

The two women eyed each other silently, as if calculating the value of an unclaimed pawn ticket. There was an unsettled feeling in the room, like something unplanned might happen.

Bess seemed to make a decision. "Maybe it's none of my business, but David is my son and I love him. Don't be like me, always guarding your heart. Be like Benny. Take a chance." She turned quickly, before Kate could speak, and hurried out the door.

Chapter 16

David found Bess standing over the kitchen sink, a carrot in one hand and a vegetable peeler in the other. He leaned in to buss her cheek. A mouthwatering aroma rose from a Dutch oven on the stove. Mona's pot roast, he thought. "Carrots?" he teased, raising an eyebrow. Mona didn't think carrots belonged in pot roast, so if Bess wanted them, she had to fix them herself. He had heard the argument a hundred times.

"Humph," she replied, rubbing where his lips had touched.

"I thought I saw your car parked over in front of the school earlier today," he hinted. He didn't really expect an answer. When none came, he tried another tactic.

"I heard you offered Benny one of the puppies for finding McCreery. That was kind."

"Not really. He wants McCreery."

"If he keeps the puppy that looks like McCreery, the two of you could take him to a couple of dog shows, find out what the puppy's made of." He tried to sound indifferent but failed.

"That's not going to happen. I'm perfectly happy being retired." She dropped the carrot into the Dutch oven and wiped her hands on a towel. Signaling him to follow, she led the way into the living room. She slid into her favorite

Queen Anne chair beside the fireplace.

He lifted a magazine off the matching chair opposite hers and flapped it at her. "*Dog World*?"

She dropped her eyes. "I've been meaning to cancel my subscription. Been so busy I haven't gotten around to it."

He sat and crossed his legs, as if he intended to stay awhile. He ran his eyes over his mother's uncombed hair and carelessly buttoned shirt but kept his observations to himself.

She broke the silence. "I'm beginning to think your Aunt Mona's not moving to Florida after all."

"Really?" He barely concealed a grin. He had predicted many times the two sisters would never be able to live that far apart.

"She claims one thing after another's not finished in her condo, but I can tell she's making excuses."

He leaned across the empty space and picked a strip of carrot off her shirt sleeve. "Really, Mother. How are you getting along?"

"Fine, thank you very much. Not a single dog in sight." She swept her arm past several unwashed coffee mugs, a stack of unopened bills, and a couple of old Christmas catalogues crowding the coffee table. Her hand halted in mid-arc. McCreery had chosen that moment to come padding through the door with his toy fish in his mouth.

David raised his eyebrows.

"Oh, for heaven's sake! McCreery doesn't count. He's a member of the family."

McCreery pushed his fish into David's hand and stared hopefully. David gave it a toss, and McCreery ran to retrieve it. Apparently, once was enough because the dog settled down beside Bess, his chin resting on her foot.

"McCreery's still got a lot of life left in him," David said, giving him the once-over. "He might be good for a few more trophies."

She pulled her thick eyebrows into a warning frown.

He held up his hands in mock surrender. “Okay, I give.” He sat back and so did she.

“So, why are you here?”

His face softened. “I’ve been thinking about you, Mother. How special you are.”

She studied a stain on the Oriental rug. When she spoke, her gravelly voice was almost a whisper, “I wasn’t cut out to be a mother. It’s a wonder I didn’t ruin you altogether. I have to give Mona credit for that.”

He leaned closer. “Mona helped, but you were my mother. Talking to the boy has made me remember.”

He held out a hand, but she hoisted herself out of her chair as if she hadn’t seen, coughing something back. She snapped her fingers. “Come, McCreery,” she called too loudly, perhaps not noticing he was stretched out at her feet. “That dog’s so spoiled he has to be reminded to pee.” She glanced at her son. “You can stay for supper if you want. Pot roast — with carrots!”

Chapter 17

The Danbury Kiwanis had set up a treasure hunt for this week's Funhouse Friday, and Benny and Steffie were a team. In honor of the occasion, she had dressed like a pirate in a long black skirt, a white blouse with puffy sleeves, and a red bandana around her neck. Two gold hoop earrings hung down to her shoulders. Benny had tied a neon blue scarf borrowed from Sonya's underwear drawer around his head and stuck a black patch over one eye. The two of them had been the first to figure out the clues because he knew every inch of the school, and she was good at finding the hidden meaning in the words. They were sitting outside on the picnic bench waiting for the others to catch up. She shoved the popcorn bowl closer to him, but he shook his head.

"You feeling all right?" she asked with a worried frown.

He shrugged, but a small smile twitched at the corners of his mouth. He lowered his voice dramatically. "I took a personal holiday yesterday and went to the top of Gallows Hill Road." He reached into his pocket and took out a tattered piece of something that might once have been rope. With a fiendish grin, he tossed it at her like a snake.

"Gotcha!"

She jumped back, nearly tipping over her chair. When the snake didn't move, she straightened her bandana and gave him a withering look. "So puerile."

He rolled his bottom lip and hung his head. "Sorry, Steffie. That was lame. I found McCreery, but not on Gallows Hill."

Her angry look vanished. "Really? You found him just like in the dream?"

He dropped his chin. "Yes, but it didn't turn out the way I thought. He picked Bess."

Her face grew serious. "Gee, Benny. I'm sorry."

"And that's not all. Bess was so guilty she tried to give me a puppy that looks exactly like McCreery. He's practically a famous champion. At least he will be soon."

"So what's the problem?"

"He's a poodle, and besides, my dad won't let me have a dog."

"Poodles are the world's smartest dogs." She winced, apparently remembering he could be sensitive about the topic of brains.

This time he didn't mind. "You're right. The puppy is pretty smart, and he doesn't look that much like a poodle."

"A puppy's a big decision, but you'll figure something out. Isn't that what your meetings with Dr. Kate are for? To solve big problems?"

"Good idea. I'll bring it up at our meeting Monday."

"Whatever you decide, I'm proud of you for finding McCreery."

Benny's insides melted like butter on a hot scone. His toes and fingers tingled, as if waking from a hundred years' sleep. No one had ever had so much confidence in him before, at least not a girl.

From the other end of the field, Adam signaled and pointed to where the other students had gathered. The treasure hunt was over. Benny grabbed his backpack and slung it over his shoulder. Something fell out and clattered to the floor. It rolled under the table.

He and Steffie reached at the same time. She grabbed it first. She held up a prescription bottle full of bright blue pills. "What are you doing with these?" she gasped.

His face turned red. He grabbed the bottle from her hand. "Mind your own business." He stuffed the bottle in his pocket and ran before she could ask any more questions.

Chapter 18

Benny's oversized feet hung off the end of the couch. A big toe stuck out of one sock. His appointment was for ten thirty, but Dr. Kate wouldn't mind if he was a little early. His class was just watching a video he'd seen before, and he was worried whether Steffie had told Dr. Kate about the pills. It was hard to know what a girl dressed like a lollipop might do, but today Steffie wasn't his biggest worry.

As long as Dr. Kate wasn't there yet, he decided he might as well look around for some clues about her life. He didn't bother getting up off the couch. He could see the whole office just fine from where he was. Besides, she got mad the last time she caught him poking around in her things.

As usual, she hadn't left out anything personal. No family photos, no souvenirs of past vacations, no greeting cards from long-lost friends. A china tea pot in the shape of an elephant with long, painted eyelashes was the only interesting thing on a shelf full of boring books by some guy named Freud he had seen a hundred times before. He knew the elephant was Indian by the ears. He had studied the difference in science, and because it was about animals, he had no trouble remembering. In a rare slip, Dr. Kate had mentioned it had come from her grandfather in Bangalore. Her green eyes were a gift from her Irish mother.

He checked the clock on the mantle and saw he still had

a few minutes to wait. He heard a rustling under the desk. It was only Lotus repositioning herself in her dog nest. She scratched at the pillow and circled in a tight ball before heaving herself back down with an explosion of breath. He considered tossing her a wadded up homework paper to kill time, but she was already snoring. He decided to catch up on his own rest instead. He was still a growing boy and had spent most of the night tossing and turning, trying to decide about the brown puppy. Bess said it would turn out like his father McCreery, but what if it didn't? Besides, why didn't Bess keep him herself like David wanted?

Benny's eyes widened. He tapped his head with a finger. He had an idea. A true inspiration. He heard light footsteps hurrying up the stairs. He checked his watch. Ten thirty-one. It was about time she got there.

Kate hesitated in the doorway to her office. When upset, Benny had been known to shred his homework over the Oriental rug or bury a tiny china doll head first in the philodendron. The doll wore a dress that had once been yellow and said things in Benny's voice that helped her know things he couldn't say directly.

Today the office seemed in order. An oblong table with eight padded blue chairs where the teachers and therapists held their meetings took up one end of the room. The other end was decorated home-style, with a fireplace, two wingback chairs, and a three-cushioned couch where Benny was sprawled. A comfortable leather chair with an ottoman was tucked in one corner. Kate had decorated the office herself with her first paycheck after paying off her student loans. Official class photos of past students, children's artwork, and a few softening pillows added a feminine touch, but the navy, tan, and mustard color scheme was all business.

"Hello, Benny," she said, taking her usual spot. "Your teacher said you can watch the video later." She stuck a stray lock of hair back into the ornate gold clip holding her French twist in place and waited. She should have locked the clip away with the ring and her crushed hopes, but it had meant too much once to put aside altogether.

He opened one eye but said nothing. After a few moments, he squirmed uncomfortably, like the princess and the pea, and held up an empty plastic cup. Traces of chocolate pudding that matched the rim around his mouth were stuck to the sides.

The gesture reminded Kate of a much younger child and made her consider again how different Benny was from most kids at New Hope School who were extra smart. Several doctors had misdiagnosed him with ADHD because he fidgeted a lot. It was easy to miss the symptoms for anxiety without a good history, and psychotropic drugs can't cure a broken heart.

She nodded at the plastic cup. "I think that was meant for your lunch."

He rolled down his lower lip. "Sonya has me on a diet. I only had half a granola bar for breakfast."

She sighed. The boy was hungry for so much more than food. It made him stretch the truth.

"I'm sorry about McCreery. I know how much you wanted him to pick you."

He sat up and pulled a Spiderman comic book out of his backpack, withdrawing from her and the possibility of comfort.

A feeling of helplessness threatened to overwhelm her. She decided to follow his lead. "Sometimes you act like make-believe comic book characters are more important than real people. For instance, you haven't mentioned your new friend David lately."

"Daa-vid, Daa-vid," he sing-songed. "Dr. Kate has a crush on David."

She felt herself blushing. Benny had a vivid imagination

and a hunger for family that included the fantasy that she and David would get together. She was sorry he would be disappointed again.

Benny thumbed through his comic for a minute, jiggling his foot the way he did when he was worried. She realized he had something important to say.

"My dad says I might not be having meetings much longer. He thinks I'm doing great," he said without looking up.

A shiver ran down her spine. Parents often pulled their children out of treatment at the first sign of progress. It was one of the heartbreaks of her work. She might love the children she worked with and be privy to their feelings, but their futures and their hearts belonged elsewhere. In the end, she always had to say good-bye. Sometimes it happened at the worst possible time, like now.

"I'll give him a call, but your dad's the boss. We only have meetings if he says so," she said, trying to keep the worry out of her voice. Children experience a loyalty conflict any time they bring up a concern about their parents. Benny had taken a risk by giving her a heads-up.

He wriggled in his seat and tugged at a wedgie. "Actually, I've been thinking."

"Really?" she asked absently, wondering how to approach Benny's dad. He wasn't a bad father, just more caught up in his own wishes than his son's. Maybe someday he would be proud of Benny for what he could do instead of focusing on what he couldn't.

"Yeah, I might be getting a puppy." He paused, waiting for her reaction.

She tried to keep her voice neutral. "A puppy? That's interesting. You used to say McCreery was the only dog you'd ever love. What changed your mind?"

He flipped his hands out at his sides. "McCreery, of course. He loves both me and Bess, and I figured if a dog could love two people, a boy could love two dogs."

Kate smiled to herself. He had taken a big step. The solution she had mentioned to Bess was already happening. He could learn to love a dog of his own and love McCreery, too. Maybe someday he would even let go of his mom the same way. Someday.

He stood and began pacing. "Everyone says McCreery used to be the greatest show dog in the world. He even could've won Westminster if Bess had given him the chance." He shot a hard look at Kate.

She leaned forward, afraid she could guess where he was heading. "Go on."

"There's this puppy that looks a lot like him. For example, they're both brown. I'm thinking about taking him to Westminster. My mother would really be impressed."

She shifted uncomfortably. For a minute, she had hoped he might actually be thinking about himself, but no. It was his mother, always his mother. "So you want the puppy to impress your mother, not because you like him?"

He stuck his fingers in his ears. "I'm not listening. La-la-la-la."

She suppressed an angry sigh. His mother loved him in her own self-absorbed way, but she would always put herself first. As his psychoanalyst, her job was to help him accept that and move on, but so far she hadn't succeeded. The boy was an endless fount of schemes to win his mother's attention that inevitably ended in failure. There was the black belt in karate that ended when he took a swing at someone, the skateboard championship that collapsed when he tripped and bloodied his elbows and knees, and the basketball trophy that shattered when a well-aimed ball knocked the wind out of him. And now this! Benny had no idea how much work it would take to qualify for a world-class show like Westminster, let alone win it. He could never manage without Bess's help. Still, crazy as it sounded, this particular idea seemed to have extra sizzle behind it.

"'Maybes' don't always come true, Benny. We've talked about that before."

He sat up, locking his fingers behind his head. "It can't be that hard. I just have to play with the puppy and teach him stuff."

"I think teaching is the important part. Besides, I thought your dad said you can't have a dog."

He rolled over so she couldn't see his face. "He's small. I'm thinking about hiding him someplace."

"I don't think that would work," she said, drumming her fingers. "A puppy needs a lot of care. Besides, you'll need help with the training."

"David will help me. He promised."

She hadn't expected that. "Are you sure?"

"David is like me. He loves making his mother happy. He thinks taking the puppy to Westminster would be the perfect hobby for her old age. She's wanted to win her whole life but never went before. Nobody knows why."

Kate glanced at the clock. With Benny's limited attention span, it was helpful to meet frequently in shorter sessions. "Our meeting is almost over. We'll talk more about this next time."

He clasped his hands together prayer-like. "Five extra minutes?"

It would be easy to give in, but children with complicated attachments to their mothers needed help separating. She needed to stay firm. "Is it good-bye forever or just until tomorrow?"

"Tomorrow," he muttered under his breath. He picked up his backpack and shuffled to the door. She came around and stood in front of him. Last fall, they had stood eye to eye. Now he was half a foot taller.

He looked at the floor. "Do you think my mother's proud of me?" His voice was so small, she almost didn't hear.

She struggled to keep her voice even. "What do you think?"

His bottom lip trembled, and he didn't answer.

She stood quietly, waiting, not wanting to undermine him when he was trying to act manfully.

He hoisted his backpack and started down the stairs. Halfway down, he began whistling one of those tunes from a band with a funny name she never could remember. All the kids loved it.

He turned to see if she was watching.

She was there, looking down. She whispered something softly to herself, like a blessing.

He smiled and gave a thumbs-up. "Don't worry, Dr. Kate. Everything will work out. You'll see. Everything will be super fine."

⚜⚜⚜

"A dog?" Sonya squeaked, wiggling her nose like a weasel. "A boy who can't remember to empty the dishwasher can't take care of a dog."

Benny's dad looked up over the top of his reading glasses long enough to tell his son, "Listen to your stepmother."

Chapter 19

Bess turned the page on her desk calendar and scratched an "X" through the date with the big red circle. Today the puppies were a full three months old, and she could let them go. Some breeders separated the puppies from their mothers at six weeks, but eager as she was to have this job behind her, she never let a puppy leave that young. The extra time with the mother made a better dog for life: calmer, more trusting, ready to learn. It was the same for both show dogs and pets.

She pulled back the curtain and peeked through the gap into the breaking dawn. Just as she thought, Hannah was pacing in front of the puppy shed. A white van with "Hannah's Own Kennels" written in black letters was parked to one side. Six puppy-sized crates were stacked and waiting by the tailgate. Hannah's hands twisted nervously in front of her, and Bess concluded there was no lingering pain from the wrist she had broken three months earlier. At six feet tall, with steel-colored braids tied across the top of her head, she was one of Redding's few African Americans and bent her neck to no one. Her family had arrived generations ago at the home of a Quaker family by way of the Underground Railroad, making her more of a native than most of the so-called Yankees who wore their heritage like a badge of honor.

Bess checked the bedside clock. Five minutes to six in the morning. She didn't intend to be one minute early or one minute late, either. At age fifty, Hannah had been waiting twenty years to become the top poodle breeder in the country. She could wait another five minutes.

Bess patted her hair into place and examined her face in the mirror. No telltale dark circles from a sleepless night, no red swollen eyes. The ice packs had done their job, not to mention Mona's expensive creams. Even so, just to be sure, she had rubbed on some borrowed concealer. She couldn't bear for Hannah to know what today was costing her. In building the kennel of her dreams, she had constructed herself along with it. The eighteen-hour days, the ledgers that balanced on a wing and a prayer, even the puppies whose promise fizzled when they hit adolescence were as much a part of herself as her own flesh, blood, and bone. Letting go of Umpawaug Kennels was letting go of herself.

Not that she had ever thought the task would be easy. She had read somewhere that one could be inoculated against something unpleasant, even traumatic, by rehearsing it over and over, and she embraced the idea wholeheartedly. For almost a decade, she had been picturing today in her mind's eye. She had let her imagination run over the empty puppy shed, the barren field where the kennels once stood, the silence that would greet her when she opened the front door. Now that the actual day had arrived, her rehearsals seemed pitifully naïve. Was it possible she had mistaken the problem all along? Maybe the challenge wasn't letting go of the past but facing up to what came next. For that, she was utterly unprepared.

It was the brown puppy's fault. Until he had come along, she had resigned herself to the inevitable. Nothing could stop Hannah's Own from becoming the new top kennel in the country for standard poodles, and that was just fine.

But now, unexpectedly, the old ambition she had tucked away so neatly was stirring again. If only the puppy weren't so very like his father. Still, this was no time to waver. She couldn't handle a dog in the ring herself anymore and hiring a handler wasn't for her. She had never done it before, and she wasn't about to start now. Besides, no matter how tempting the little fellow was, until he passed through adolescence, no one could be sure how he would look in maturity.

Still, one question circled round and round in her brain. Why had she agreed to that last breeding with McCreery? Surely, she wasn't hoping for one final try at Best in Show at Westminster. No, that was ridiculous.

She picked up the envelopes containing the AKC registration forms filled out in her flowery script. "Umpawaug" was recorded as the kennel name the way she and Hannah agreed when she had sold Susie. That way, McCreery's last litter of puppies would be tied to her kennel forever. The space for the owner's name was left blank, so Hannah could sell the puppies or keep them herself. She shuffled the envelopes and counted them again to be sure. Yes, six. It was all right. She was safe.

She stepped through the back door, hands on hips, as though she had been the one kept waiting. She walked briskly, shoulders straight, as if she didn't have a care in the world. When she reached Hannah, she tipped her hand toward the puppy shed door. "You know where they are. It's not like you haven't been here before."

Hannah hesitated. Bess ought to lead the way. It was almost like Bess was forcing her into the position of usurper. Still, there was no point in arguing. Hannah stepped inside. The puppies scratched eagerly at the sides of the whelping pen, barely large enough to hold them all now, and set off an excited chorus. To her ears, it sounded like a welcoming cheer.

Bess had a different explanation. "They're hungry. I didn't feed them this morning. I figured you wouldn't want a bunch of puppies yerping all over your nice, clean van."

Hannah knew Bess was hiding her hurt behind gruff words. She regretted that her windfall came from Bess's loss, but the prospect of the future lightened her guilt. She began to feel almost giddy. Her eyes rested on the brown boy who looked so much like his father. Instinctively, she knew he was Bess's favorite. McCreery had enjoyed the most spectacular show career of any dog in Umpawaug history, and this puppy resembled him closely.

Hannah didn't need to choose among the six puppies, but if she had to pick just one, it would be the robust black fellow staring up at her with hungry eyes. He seemed to say he could hardly wait to start winning. As if to underscore the point, he gave his brown brother a solid bump, hind end to hind end, and dislodged him from the front of the pack. She leaned into the whelping pen and scooped him up. She tucked him under her arm and reached for his brown brother. The little fellow scooted backwards, just beyond her fingertips. His bobbed tail was wagging, so he was playing with her. Still, it made her think. Perhaps she should try one more time to convince Bess to keep him. She hoped someone would do the same for her when her time came. She decided to leave him for last.

As if seeing through Hannah's plan, Bess busied herself by gathering up the last of the puppy paraphernalia. The other four puppies bunched together, paws scratching excitedly at the side of the box.

Hannah sighed, uncertain what words would suffice for such a poignant occasion. Still, it wasn't in her nature to let the moment pass unremarked. "My heart goes out ..." she began in a choked voice. Before she could finish, the door flung open and Benny burst in like the king's messenger.

"I've changed my mind. I'll take him!" He hiked up his

pants with a pleased grin and looked at the two women for approval.

Hannah gripped the black puppy tighter and glared at Bess. What kind of stunt was she trying to pull? "Whom does the boy think he's taking exactly?" she asked in a thin voice.

Benny's eyes shot to the black puppy in her arms, the temper that had brought him to New Hope School threatening to explode. He turned to Bess. "You said I could have any puppy I wanted for saving McCreery's life. Don't tell me you forgot?"

Bess paled. She remembered all right. She had made the promise in the heat of the moment and regretted it almost instantly, but he had steadfastly refused her offer, so it didn't seem to matter. And now this, at the last possible moment. A puppy was an awesome responsibility, one the boy wasn't ready for. Still, if he hadn't found McCreery ...

She couldn't bear to think of it.

She studied Benny's face carefully. The hunger in his eyes reminded her of another boy and other promises made, and broken, thirty-odd years ago. Whatever his reason for changing his mind, the puppy was important to him.

She turned to Hannah. "It's true. I promised. I'm entitled to pick of the litter, and the boy can choose for me. Go ahead, Benny, pick the puppy you want." She leaned against the counter and crossed her ankles nonchalantly, as if his decision was of no greater significance than what she would have for dinner that night. Meryl Streep would have envied the performance.

Hannah pulled the black boy closer and told Bess in a firm voice, "If even one of these puppies turns out like his father, the Umpawaug legacy will continue another generation. At their age, even you can't be sure which one it will be. Surely you're not going to give a puppy of such immense potential to an inexperienced child."

Benny puffed out his cheeks, but Bess silenced him with a glare. Hannah was correct, but Benny would soon tire of the work involved in caring for a puppy, and then she could send the puppy to Hannah. She would still be safe.

"No, not exactly. The boy and I will co-own the dog. The puppy will stay here with me until Benny is ready to take care of him himself. We'll work out the financial details later. Who pays for what, etcetera."

Benny jerked up his head. Finances were an aspect he hadn't considered, but he pushed his doubts aside in the desire of the moment. As long as Bess kept the puppy at her place, Sonya and his dad couldn't say a word. It was the perfect solution. He made an "I told you so" face at Hannah. "That's more like it," he said.

He leaned back for a better view of the puppies and rubbed his chin the way his dad did when he had a tough choice to make. The puppies were thrilled by this exciting new person's attention and squirmed and bumped their little butts against each other to get closer. He took his time, enjoying the drama too much to be rushed. He seemed about to choose, then hesitated. "What if I decide to enter the puppy in dog shows and stuff?"

Bess jerked back her head. She thought the boy wanted a pet, not a show dog. The prospect of watching a clumsy boy make a mess of handling Breaker was more painful than giving up on dog shows herself.

She forced herself to take a calming breath. She had nothing to worry about. The boy would never be able to manage on his own. "That's up to you. Just don't expect me to help," she said.

Hannah's mouth opened and a mocking laugh rumbled out. She nodded at Benny who had collapsed in the only chair while his elders stood. "That boy? Turn an obstreperous puppy into a show dog?"

A hush fell over the room. Benny's face flushed red, but

before he could react, Bess pointed at the puppies jostling together at the edge of the pen. "Go ahead. Choose."

He gave Hannah another dirty look and leaned into the whelping box. This time the brown boy pushed to the front of the pack, scratching and whimpering to be chosen, but Benny still wasn't ready. The tip of his tongue showed between his teeth as he studied them one by one.

He turned to Bess, avoiding Hannah's eye. "Which one do you like?"

Bess stepped back, waving her hand. "Oh, no, you don't. It's your call."

He didn't know it, but she was giving him good advice. If he were to have a prayer of beating the odds and turning the puppy into a champion, he and the dog would need a strong bond connecting them.

Hannah gave a little gasp when he started to reach for the black boy in her arms, but then he remembered the brown boy was the one who had jumped out of the box and run toward him the day he had first seen the puppies. The black one had held back. Maybe the brown boy was best.

As if reading Benny's mind, the brown boy scratched harder at the sides imprisoning him. He squeezed his forehead into a small frown and gave a high-pitched, sharp whine. He was begging Benny to choose him.

No way could Benny resist love like that. Every blue rubber band on his braces stretched into a crescent moon smile. "If I can't have McCreery, I'll take this one," he announced and hefted the puppy onto his shoulder. The puppy seemed pleased and licked Benny's chin excitedly.

Hannah exhaled slowly but kept her arms wrapped tightly around her favorite.

Now that Benny had made his choice, his temper cooled toward Hannah. "I'm naming mine Breaker because he'll be a record breaker. What about you?"

"His call name will be Chicory," Hannah replied without

hesitation, as if she had been thinking about it for a while.

He lost his concentration trying to remember if chicory was something good to eat, and Breaker wriggled out of his arms. The puppy slid to the floor and began running in circles between the three pairs of human legs, tail whirring like a fan on a hot summer's day.

"That one's going to be a handful," Hannah predicted.

An affectionate smile twitched at the corners of Bess's mouth. "Just like his father." Then she remembered herself. "Catch that puppy, Benny, and put him back where he belongs."

Grabbing the squirming puppy under his belly, Benny dropped him into the whelping pen. With a heavy sigh, he fell onto the rusty metal chair with his legs outstretched. "Puppies sure are a lot of work."

Hannah and Bess exchanged knowing smiles. "It'll be like old times being back in the ring together," Hannah said, still grinning.

Bess scowled and held up her hands. "Why can't people get it through their heads? I'm finished, finito, done. The boy and I will be co-owners. That's all. Breaker can stay here in the puppy shed, and Benny can visit whenever he wants. It'll be his job to take care of him after school." She pulled the AKC registrations from her pocket and counted out five. She held back the sixth and handed the others to Hannah.

Benny watched silently from his chair as Hannah and Bess left with four squirming puppies tucked under their arms. The fifth followed closely behind, not wanting to be forgotten. Breaker remained alone in the whelping pen, like the last patron in an empty theater. The thump of his tail was the only sound in the room.

Benny leaned into the box and pulled out his new puppy with one hand. Gently, he placed him down on the floor. The little fellow stood on his hind legs and scratched excitedly at

Benny's leg, wriggling with unrestrained happiness. Benny had never felt so important in his life. He clasped his hands over his stomach and nodded slowly, as if he had worked out a thorny problem. "I've thought a lot about it, Breaker, and I've decided we can be best friends, even if you are a poodle. McCreery's my first best friend because I saved his life, and you can be my second best friend."

Breaker grabbed Benny's shoelace and gave it a good yank, as if he understood he had been given second place to his father and didn't intend to remain there. Benny lifted the squirming mass of muscle and warm puppy smell and held him close against his chest. Delighted, Breaker slurped Benny's face and neck with a tongue that seemed as long as he was. Benny's eyes closed in dreamy happiness. He was on his way to Westminster. So what if Bess wouldn't help him. How hard could it be? He'd get right on it — first thing tomorrow.

Chapter 20

After months of heavy wool coats and gray skies, Kate couldn't resist the perfect first day of May. She shoved the notes from her last session into the file drawer and draped a light sweater over her shoulders. Lotus heard the hopeful sounds and scrambled out from underneath the desk. They headed for the wooden swing hanging off the maple tree, and Kate sat, dragging her feet along the spot the students had worn down in the grass. The sun was warm on her face, urging her to close her eyes and rest for a minute.

She must have nodded off because Lotus's sharp barks jerked her awake. She opened her eyes to find David and Breaker standing over her. Maybe her guard was down because it was springtime and she was still half-asleep, but she felt magnanimous and willing to overlook the way their last meeting had ended. She didn't know many accountants, but it was hard to picture him hunched over a thick ledger like Scrooge, not with that cleft chin and those dimples at the tips of a welcoming smile.

The dogs were glad to be out in the fine spring day as well. Lotus's feathered tail swept back and forth, eyes fixed on the handsome brown puppy at the end of David's lead. Breaker's bobbed tail whirred, and his nose quivered with excitement. The two sped off in a game of chase.

David took a long, quiet look at the campus. "I've never heard of a school before that helps children with their feelings. It's got to be rough on your own emotions sometimes."

She tried to hide her surprise. It wasn't often someone thought about her work from her point of view. "It can be. We've been known to keep children with serious emotional problems out of mental hospitals."

"Really? Little kids get admitted to mental hospitals?"

"Unfortunately. More often, they're put on a bunch of psychotropic drugs that nobody ever tested on children."

David shuddered. "I'm glad Benny's not on any pills. He was boasting about it the other day."

Kate's eyes knitted in a little frown. "Really? I wonder what brought that on."

"He said he was on two different medicines before he came to your school, but you got him off them."

Kate couldn't comment on Benny's treatment, so she studied her shoe.

David seemed to understand. "You have so much passion for what you do. You remind me of my mother when she talks about her dogs, or at least the way she used to." He clapped his hand over his mouth. "Oops, I guess I shouldn't mention my mother to a Freudian."

She laughed, and he laughed, too. Then she added seriously, "It's not easy helping children like Benny. I'm sorry I didn't trust you before about Benny keeping Breaker, but he wanted the puppy for all the wrong reasons. I was afraid he'd get hurt."

David met her gaze. "I'm more of an expert on kids getting hurt than you can imagine."

The emotion in his voice went straight to her heart, but Benny was her responsibility. "Then you understand my concern. I don't want his heart to get broken again."

He straightened his cap. "I want that, too. Benny's

told me his dad has forbidden him to see his mother as a punishment for stealing money out of his wallet. He wanted to buy her a birthday present." He saw the color rise in her cheeks. "You probably knew that already," he said sheepishly.

Her voice was tense. "I thought we understood each other. Benny is my responsibility."

"He asked me to speak to you. He was hoping you could persuade his father to let him see on her birthday."

She rose, ramrod straight. "You don't get it. Benny's got to learn to speak for himself. We've been working on that for weeks."

He lowered his eyes. "I wasn't trying to interfere," he said quickly. "I was worried Benny might have taken the money for something he's hiding. Kids his age sometimes buy stuff they think is cool, but isn't." He could feel her eyes burning into him, and he gave it his last shot, "I watch the evening news and know what can happen."

She started to say something, he wasn't sure what, but just then the dogs charged around the corner, barreling toward them.

"I'm supposed to meet Benny tomorrow morning, so we can begin training Breaker. We're hoping to enter him in a dog show in a few weeks. Do I at least have your blessing for that?" he asked, his hurt showing in spite of himself.

For a long moment, she didn't answer. Then she nodded.

"Fine," he said and offered a small smile. He still hoped the rift between them wouldn't be permanent.

She turned to leave.

He held out a hand. "Wait, I'll walk you back to your office."

If she agreed, another invitation would follow. "Thank you, anyway," she said and turned away. Lotus gave Breaker a lingering look and followed.

Chapter 21

Benny hoped to catch Steffie before she left, but when he reached the bench she was nowhere in sight. A stranger was seated on the bench where he expected her to be, and from what he had seen in the movies, she looked exactly like a hippie flower child, right down to the daisy behind her ear. Only this girl didn't seem all full of peace and love. Her stringy dark hair hung down around her face like a shield, and she was worrying a hangnail. She gave him a quick look. The flower child was Steffie.

His heart sank to the pit of his stomach. What had happened to his little lollipop girl? Still, he needed to find out if she had told anyone about the bottle of pills. "Mom late?" he asked, stalling to work up his courage.

Her hair swung back and forth in a "no" but she didn't speak. Maybe she thought it was none of his business. She crossed her legs, and he noticed a pair of cool red-and-silver hightops that didn't exactly go with the rest of her outfit. He had been begging Sonya for a pair just like them for months, only for boys.

"Mine, neither," he said, glad it was true for once.

She stood and began swinging her arms in wide circles. "This school is weird. Kids get away with a ton of stuff they never would at a real school. Eric H. kept his head on his desk the entire math period today, and Mrs. Siemers didn't do a thing just because he's supposed to be upset over a cat dying or something. It wasn't even a real cat, just something he saw on TV."

Benny knew Eric wasn't upset about a cat. His little brother had some awful disease and was as bald as a hard-boiled egg. No one knew if he would get better. "Mrs. Siemers isn't as dumb as you think. I'm not crazy about regular teachers myself, but the teachers here are different. They like kids like us. Otherwise, they'd be nuts to work here." He grinned. "Face it. They have to put up with me."

She shrugged. "Maybe, but my mother'll pull me out again, anyway. It's kind of a hobby with her."

He felt sorry for her, but he had his own problems. He stuck his hands in his pockets and stood with his legs apart like the rock star his mother liked. "Say, you didn't mention anything about that bottle to anyone, did you?" His voice quavered a little, and he hoped she wouldn't notice.

She met his eyes. "Duh."

She hadn't exactly said no, but he decided his secret was safe for now. He exhaled a long breath. "Thanks."

She donned a serious face that looked a lot like Dr. Kate's. "You shouldn't be fooling around with drugs."

He hated disappointing her, but he had no choice. "It's not what you think. Besides, someone dressed like a flower child shouldn't talk."

The stretch limo glided to a stop in front of them, and he watched her slide into the backseat. She gave a little wave, and his heart grew lighter. Maybe she wasn't that mad after all. Maybe she understood. A good feeling rose up inside. His whole body tingled. She had kept his secret. They were partners, secret agents on special assignment. He could hardly wait for tomorrow to see her again.

⚜ ⚜ ⚜

Sonya thrust an arm through the Corvette window. A piece of paper dangled from the tips of two fingers. "Look at this. Fifty-seven on a math test. I found it crumpled up in an empty potato chip bag in his lunch box — as if stealing from your wallet weren't bad enough."

Benny's dad cut the engine and loosened his tie. "I thought he was supposed to be in his room doing homework every afternoon." He grabbed his briefcase from the backseat and headed toward the door. "Get that doctor of his on the phone. I intend to get to the bottom of this."

Chapter 22

Benny dangled a bit of glazed donut left over from breakfast above Breaker's head. "No, sit," he shouted, like people do when they are trying to make foreigners understand English. It didn't work any better on the puppy. Breaker leaped for the donut and grazed it with the end of his tongue before it landed on the ground. Benny studied it carefully for dog germs and ate it himself.

David groaned. The Housatonic dog show was just weeks away. Breaker could just qualify for the six months age requirement, but at this rate he wouldn't be prepared.

"Shall we try that again?" he asked with a weary sigh.

Benny glared at him. "*We're* finished, but you can try if you want."

David silently warned himself to be patient. Teaching Breaker a few basic manners was harder than he ever imagined. Good thing help was on its way. Jim and Holly Wren had trained almost as many poodles as Bess.

"You almost had it that time," David encouraged. "One more try."

Benny dropped down onto the grass. "Bess has the right idea. I'm thinking of retiring myself." Now that he thought of it, he hadn't paid her a visit lately. He had caught her sneaking out of the puppy shed a couple of times when he was early picking up Breaker, but she had hurried away without speaking.

David sat beside him and asked calmly, “If you give up now, what’ll happen to Breaker? You can’t just say you want a puppy one minute and throw him out the next.”

Benny lifted his eyes in a cool stare. “Why not? People do it to kids all the time.”

David took a deep breath. “Breaker loves you. Doesn’t that mean anything?”

Benny hadn’t expected that. He shifted his gaze to Breaker. The puppy was shaking a chew toy back and forth like a dead rat and making pleased puppy growls. Breaker felt Benny’s eyes on him and hurried over, his tail whirring with pleasure at being noticed.

Benny wrapped his arm around the puppy’s neck. “Don’t worry, big guy. You’re safe with me.”

David nodded, satisfied the crisis had passed. “See if you can get Breaker to heel,” he said, but the boy’s attention had wandered to a different dog. McCreery had slipped quietly into their little group. He made a wide circle, came to a stop, stood at attention, and circled again. His pink-and-lime stuffed fish stuck out of both sides of his mouth. Obviously, he thought he looked rather fetching.

Benny wrinkled his nose. “What’s McCreery doing?” He pointed at his own head and drew a corkscrew in the air. “Do you think he has mental problems or something? You can tell me. Some of the kids at my school do, so I’m used to it.”

David smothered a laugh and studied the dog more closely. McCreery still wasn’t back to one hundred percent of his old self, but his coat was thick, his almond-shape eyes were bright with a lively intelligence, and his gait was as elegant as a gazelle’s.

“If you ask me, he’s practicing for the show ring.”

Benny gripped his waist and spat out a hearty guffaw. “Good one.”

"No, really, he's been doing it for years. If I didn't know better, I'd say he's staying in shape in case his time ever comes. Even my Aunt Mona doesn't understand why my mother never gave him a chance."

Benny's jaw dropped. "You mean for Westminster?" He took a second look. McCreery's close-cropped coat was nothing like the photos taken back in the day when he was a famous champion. "I'm not sure."

McCreery tossed his head, nose in air as if highly insulted, and made the circle again.

"He could use a haircut, but if ever a dog deserved a chance at Westminster, it was McCreery," David explained.

Breaker had listened to enough talk about his father and gave an impatient, sharp puppy bark. He had almost reached his full size and looked more like his sire than ever. The proud thrust of his chest and his regal head — when he was quiet long enough to show them off — were qualities that had made his father a champion when he was almost the same age.

McCreery sat, scratching an errant itch behind his ear, and dropped his toy fish on the ground. Seeing his chance, Breaker dashed in and snatched it away. He made fast circles around McCreery, tossing his head with a wide grin that said, "Come get me."

"Oh, oh," Benny said, leaping to his feet. "This isn't going to be pretty."

McCreery let out a low growl and stayed where he was. That's all it took. Breaker dropped the fish like it was made of hot chili peppers and huddled behind Benny, tail tucked in. McCreery gave a disdainful look at the cowering puppy and picked up the prize in his mouth.

David smiled. "McCreery's still top dog. Now, let's see if you can get this puppy back on track."

Benny slipped a couple of dog biscuits out of his pocket, tossed one to McCreery, and shouted "Sit!" at Breaker. The puppy dropped like a stone, quivering with excitement. He took the biscuit gently from Benny's hand, but his good behavior lasted only as long as the flavor. He gave a shrill bark, tail vibrating with anticipation. Clearly, he thought he deserved another. McCreery gave a disgusted snort, or maybe it was only a sneeze, and padded off.

"Looks like the puppy's winning," a man's voice boomed.

David looked up with a smile. A middle-aged man and a woman were heading toward them. They were both thin and of medium height. The man had salt-and-pepper hair; hers was dark and hung in a neat pageboy. A silk scarf sporting a famous signature hung loosely around her neck and matched the aubergine and navy in her husband's tie.

David waved his hand toward Benny like the maître d' at a fancy restaurant showing a good tipper to his favorite table. "Holly, Jim, this is Benny Neusner, the young man I've been telling you about. Benny, meet Holly Wren and Dr. Jim Wren. They've bred a kennel full of champion standard poodles themselves and have offered to give us a few tips."

Benny remembered his manners and shook hands with them both. He gave Jim a careful look. "Don't tell me you're another meeting doctor?"

Jim smiled. "No such luck. Mostly head colds and flu." He turned to David. "We saw McCreery heading back home just now. Did you ever find out who stole him?"

David shook his head. "The only clue was a van with a dented fender on the right front, and that's not much to go on."

Jealous he wasn't in the spotlight, Breaker wriggled and pulled on his lead, eager to meet the company.

"It's okay. You can let him go, Benny," David said.

"You sure? He's got his ADHD really bad this morning."

Breaker ran back and forth between Holly and Jim,

tail hidden, butt wriggling. He was so beside himself, he piddled on the tooled leather flap decorating the top of Jim's shoe. Benny was sure some cuss words he had never heard before would follow, but Jim took a handkerchief out of his breast pocket and dried his shoe.

A breeze lifted the end of Holly's beautiful silk scarf and caught Breaker's eye. Wouldn't a game of capture the flag be fun?

"No!" Benny hollered.

Breaker pressed his belly against the grass and covered his eyes with his paws, in a passable imitation of regret. He lay quietly for a moment, then removed one paw, and peeked at Benny impishly. Benny grinned back.

David stuck his unlit pipe in his mouth the way he did when he was worried. He turned to the Wrens. "Do you think he'll settle down enough for the show ring?"

"The boy or the dog?" Jim asked in a stage whisper.

Holly frowned at Jim, but she was smiling, too. "Poodles are supposed to be lively. It's in the standard." Her musical voice might have belonged to an opera star.

Benny puffed out his chest. "Yeah, lively. You could say that."

Jim scrunched down and held his hand out to the puppy. "Come, boy," he called firmly. Breaker approached slowly, head down. Jim reached for the lead, and Breaker sprang back, grinning and wagging his tail. He ducked under Jim's arm, ran around Holly like a goal post, and snagged David's khaki pants cuff.

"He's usually not this bad," David apologized, trying to keep his dignity as he grappled with tenacious puppy teeth.

Holly bent down. "Let me try. Come, Breaker. Good boy," she called in a soothing whisper.

Lo and behold, the puppy came and sat at Holly's feet like he was planning to do it all along, if only someone would ask nicely. She reached into her pocket for a training treat and let Breaker get a whiff. Then she straightened up and jiggled the lead. "Heel!"

"Yeah, sure," Benny said under his breath. He had tried it a hundred times, and it had worked maybe twice.

Without missing a beat, Holly said in a voice like whipped cream melting on hot cocoa, "Benny, watch what I'm doing. See how I never take my eyes off him." The puppy heeled perfectly, as if he had been doing it all his life.

"No way!" Benny exclaimed. "A miracle."

Holly held up another treat and made Breaker sit prettily before getting his reward. "It's called 'baiting,'" she explained. "Breaker must learn to go into a show stance on his own. No judge wants to watch a handler constantly moving a dog's legs into position."

Jim leaned back with his arms folded, taking in every move as Holly and Breaker completed a circle. "Beautiful," he pronounced when Holly came to a halt in front of him like he was the judge at an important show. He took the lead. "Now you watch," he told his wife.

For the most part, Breaker walked politely around the imaginary ring, even if he did try to pounce on Jim's stomach when Jim told him to stay. Jim corrected him immediately with a quick jerk down on the lead. When Breaker got back in control of himself, Jim slipped him another training treat.

"That's a good trick," Benny said to no one in particular. An almost imperceptible nod passed between husband and wife, and he wondered if he would be tested next.

Jim handed Benny the lead and a couple of liver treats. "Your turn."

Benny shrugged and took the lead. "What the heck? Let's go, big fella," he shouted.

The three adults groaned at once. "Calm voice," Holly coached, but it was too late. Breaker landed with his front paws on a tender spot between Benny'

Ignoring Benny's pained expressio straight down on the lead and tell him 'N it." Benny managed to pull on the lead, bu short of a masterful command. Breaker leaped yanking Benny's arm skywards. The boy tumbled back and lay there while Breaker licked his face.

"Is Benny all right?" Holly asked with a pretty frown.

"He's fine, just playing it for all it's worth," David reassured her.

Jim glanced at David. "I'm not sure about the boy. Couldn't you handle Breaker yourself or maybe hire a professional?"

David held a warning finger to his lips. "The boy can hear like a Chihuahua." He stepped closer to the Wrens. "Bess has a soft spot for Benny. He's the only reason she kept the puppy at all. I know it sounds crazy, but I'm convinced that if she gets back in the game, it'll be because of him."

"Breaker shows all the promise of his father. I don't see how she can resist," said Holly.

Jim shifted like he had a bur in his sock. "But she knows? You're not training Breaker in secret?"

David shrugged. "Not exactly. She gave Benny permission to show him, but she never thought he could. She didn't count on me helping."

Jim and Holly exchanged worried glances. "Legally, Breaker's her dog. You can't enter him in a dog show unless she registers him," Holly said.

An ominous silence fell. No one spoke. Even Breaker froze in place.

David turned and discovered Bess standing behind him. She looked like she had just gotten out of bed, right down to her scruffy slippers. McCreery was at her side. She gave Jim and Holly a cool look and circled Breaker slowly, hands clasped rigidly behind her. Anger and pleasure struggled ominance on her face, or perhaps it was fear. Breaker ned to know something momentous was happening and od like a statue until she completed her circle. Then she rned and headed back towards her house.

For once, McCreery didn't follow. He walked purposefully up to the younger dog, head erect like a champion. It was almost like he was trying to let his son know he was still the superior dog.

Breaker lowered his head, tail swaying slowly, and waited.

Chapter 23

Standing on the front stoop of Bess's house, David spied his mother through the living room window. She was alone, so she must have sent the Wrens packing. She paced back and forth between the matching Queen Anne chairs on either side of the fireplace. Each time she made a turn, she grabbed onto their backs for support.

He rang the front doorbell.

She hesitated and began pacing again.

"I know you're in there, Mother. I'm not leaving."

She waited a minute and then swung the door open. She peered behind him. "Any more surprise visitors?"

"Only McCreery." Oddly, the old dog was waiting patiently at David's heel as if he were a guest who needed an invitation himself. "May we come in?"

She waved them inside. "Go ahead and say your piece, but it won't do any good. Holly and Jim already gave it their best shot." She sat in one of the Queen Anne chairs.

He moved to the opposite chair.

McCreery bounded up on the good sofa and circled around for the right spot. Bess threw him a warning look but let him stay. "If you're using McCreery to soften me up, think again," she said.

David felt like a chunk of suet was stuck in his throat. "Sorry, this isn't easy."

She snorted. "Glad to hear it." She squeezed her thick eyebrows together and glared at her son. "How could you encourage the boy like that, getting his hopes up for nothing? Anyone can see he'll never be able to handle a spirited dog like Breaker. The poor child can barely manage himself. And to do it behind my back. With Jim and Holly, no less!"

He leaned forward, hands folded prayer-like. "Mother, your life is a mess. You don't go out, you don't talk to people, the house is a wreck, and the way you dress? Anyone who didn't know better would think you're a bag lady."

"It's my life. What's it to you?"

He rose, arms stuck out like a battered scarecrow's. "You don't get it, do you? You haven't the faintest idea?"

"Not really."

"I'm your son. I love you." Maybe if he said it loud enough, she would hear him.

She stared at him, face blank.

He waited, but she said nothing. He spun on his heel. He had almost reached the door when she spoke.

"Wait. What do you want from me?"

He turned. Her mask was gone, leaving a defeated old woman behind. In a flood, the bitterness drained out of him. "It's not what I want *from* you, Mother. It's what I want *for* you." He stared at her for a long moment, the silence encasing them like a sprung trap. All of her muscles strained to keep her body in check and betrayed how much she wanted to give in and accept what he was offering.

"The puppy?" she asked finally, choking.

He exhaled a long sigh. He hadn't realized he had been holding his breath. He nodded. "Breaker's as good as his father. Maybe better."

Hope flickered in her eyes, danced there for a moment, and fizzled like a candle with a wet wick.

Hot blood rose in his cheeks. "Why?"

She had no answer.

He turned and left, closing the door with quiet finality.

She moved to the sofa and pulled McCreery in close. The guilty secret had been held inside too long and streamed forth in the tears running down her face.

It was true she wanted to take her dogs into the ring herself, but there was more. Even after she made up her mind to raze Umpawaug Kennels, she still planned to keep one puppy from Susie's breeding with McCreery. She told herself she needed a younger dog for company now that McCreery was getting up in years, but in her heart of hearts, she wasn't ready to give up on her dream of Westminster.

All that changed one morning last fall when she was in the kitchen fixing breakfast. McCreery was nosing around underfoot. She reached for something in the top cabinet and her trick knee gave out. She collapsed onto the floor, her leg twisted painfully underneath her. The slightest movement was excruciating, too agonizing even for tears.

Of course, McCreery thought it was a wonderful joke. They had fooled around on the floor like this hundreds of times. He pounced on her with his paws on her shoulders, grinning widely, tail wagging excitedly. Off-balance and in pain as she was, the weight of him knocked her over the rest of the way. Instinctively, she shot her hand out and slapped him. Hard! McCreery cringed and crept back into a corner. His eyes were full of pain and confusion. She never wanted a dog to look at her like that again.

Nobody had seen her. No one but McCreery knew, but she could never trust herself again. Poodles love to fool around, and when McCreery only did what was in his nature to do, she struck him. She had done it out of fear, the fear of an old woman who was only then learning what it would be like to feel helpless, too weak to get up using her own muscles. The future had risen up to meet her. She wasn't ready, but she had no choice. Puppies are all play;

they follow no rules. One minute, they are loose skin and big feet curled up on a chair looking good enough to eat, and the next, they are crawling between one's feet. She must have tripped over hundreds in her time. She couldn't take a chance, not anymore.

McCreery wriggled his head back and forth, freeing himself from her grasp. He hopped off the sofa and placed his front paws on her shoulders, sniffing her face, his touch as light as a friendly kiss. If he could have spoken, he would have told her all was forgiven the moment it happened. Instead, he lowered his head onto her lap and waited quietly until she wove her fingers through his topknot and held on for dear life.

Chapter 24

Benny was seated at the computer station chasing sharks on the screen. Every time he answered a multiplication fact correctly, one of the sharp-toothed creatures got blasted to smithereens.

"Splat! Gotcha!" he announced, looking around the room for approval. No one paid any attention. Unperturbed, he returned to the screen. He hadn't seen Kate waiting, or pretended not to.

"Can you save that for later?" she asked. She noticed he had lost a bit of baby fat in the past few weeks. Maybe he was taking his work with David and Breaker seriously and getting some much needed exercise.

"Sure. Mrs. Santos is just going to tell us about the dairies they used to have in Redding a long time ago. We learned all about it last year. I like milk and everything, but I'm not interested in seeing it squirt out of a cow, if you know what I mean."

He put the game on "pause" and waved good-bye to the other kids with a flourish. Jacob gave a halfhearted salute back without looking up from his book.

Occasionally, in nice weather, she let them have their meeting outdoors. She led them to a private spot on the deck of the main building. The lawn chairs were the old-fashioned metal kind that used to populate the front of roadside motels, only these were moss green and fresh from Millie's Plant and Garden. She got them at half-price at the end of last season when she said they were for New Hope School. She sat and Benny sat beside her.

"Summer's here," he pronounced with a big smile. He threw out his arms and sucked fresh air deep into his lungs. "You need to get a life, Dr. Kate. All you do is work. Can't you smell the flowers? Hear the birds?"

She flushed. The boy felt responsible for every grown-up he met, not to mention everything that went on in the school. It was one of the things they were working on during their meetings. "Thank you, but I can take care of myself."

He rapped his knuckles on the arm of his chair. "I haven't seen David over here lately. You don't have a new boyfriend or anything, do you?" His eyes flashed to her hands.

The third finger on her left hand, the one that had felt naked ever since she returned the engagement ring, suddenly twitched. She donned her most serious shrink face. "We're not here to talk about me, Benny."

He leaned back in his chair, surveying the grounds like they were his own particular kingdom. "Hey, where's Lotus?"

"Asleep. She's just had her walk."

He drew his mouth into a frown. "That's not good. Lotus could be pregnant. Women get tired all the time when they're having babies."

She straightened up in her chair. Usually when kids started talking about pregnancies, they'd overheard something at home. The last thing Benny needed was a new baby in his life.

He made a face. "You can breathe. Sonya's on the pill. I heard them talking."

"I see. Well, Lotus was fixed before I found her, at least I think she was, so there won't be any new puppies." Kate hoped it was true. Someone had dropped Lotus off at the school or maybe the little dog had found her own way there. Kate had looked everywhere for an owner and failed.

"You think?" Benny asked, lurching forward dramatically. "You'd better know for sure unless you want a little surprise. That's what my dad says anyway."

"Your dad's right. We don't want any surprise puppies."

"Or kids!" He puffed out his chest. "My dad says I'm more than enough."

She hid a smile. "How's the dog training coming along? You and Breaker making progress?"

He laced his fingers together and stretched his arms in front of his chest. "To tell the truth, we aren't doing so hot. Housatonic's less than three weeks away, and that puppy would rather fool around than work. Sometimes he tries to outsmart me." His eyes started to fill. "I was fine when Jim Wren was showing me what to do. David's tried, but he's not that good." He gasped, afraid he had undone his sales pitch. "About dogs, I mean. About other stuff, he's real smart."

She suppressed a sigh. Just as she had feared, Benny's hopes had outstripped his ability. "Breaker's a very energetic puppy, and you're just learning. It sounds like you could use some help."

His eyes lit up. "What about you? Lotus is a real obedient dog."

"Lotus was born with a different temperament, and she was pretty much trained when I found her. I'm afraid I don't know much about dogs. Not like Bess. If Housatonic is important to you, you know what you need to do."

"Yeah, yeah, I know. Talk to Bess myself. "

She gave a little smile. Maybe she was getting through after all.

"It won't do any good. Even David can't convince her, and he's tried, believe me."

"You're not David. They have their own issues."

"No kidding. All he thinks about is making his mother happy."

She let that one pass. Instead she said, "Even if Bess agrees, you'll be going up against some very experienced handlers. You can't let your heart get broken if you don't win. You've got to be prepared."

Benny held up both hands, palms up, like a man spinning pizza dough. "Don't worry, Dr. Kate. I'm prepared. No problem at all."

Chapter 25

Now that Benny was standing on Bess's doorstep, his stomach was twisted like a pretzel. It didn't help that the house was dark and lonely-looking, the sort of place where a person could get swallowed up and disappear forever. He bent his neck back as far as it would go so he could see the turret rising into the night sky. There was a small window with diamond-shaped panes, and he thought he could see two yellow-green eyes staring out at him. Maybe his imagination was running wild, but he was glad Dr. Kate had said Lotus could come along for company.

He looked down at the little dog sitting calmly at his heel and his racing heart slowed a little. To be on the safe side, maybe he should come back tomorrow before the sun went down. He started to back away, but Lotus stood on her hind legs and scratched the door eagerly. A moment later, it opened. McCreery's nose stuck through the crack.

"Come in," Bess said, holding the door open.

He hesitated.

"It's all right. The little dog can come in, too. She and McCreery are great friends, but I don't know her name."

This was a good start. He knew something she didn't. Maybe things would go his way after all. He flashed the smile he had been practicing in the mirror and said, "Lotus, Lotus Kumar."

Lotus wiggled her hind end and panted excitedly. McCreery seemed as pleased as Lotus about the visit. He tossed his head in the direction of the stairs, and the two dogs raced each other upstairs, a route they apparently knew well.

She turned to him. "So, what dirty work has David sent you to do this time?"

He had never seen anybody flick her eyelashes so fast before. "I'm sorry you're too old for dog shows and everything, but I'm not and I've decided I want to be in this one called Housatonic. You might have heard of it."

She peered over her reading glasses like he was as welcome as a toothache. "Housatonic? You and that puppy dog? Tell David he's got to do better than that."

He jiggled his leg and his cheeks turned red. "No, really, it's my idea. I reee-ally want to go."

"Well, good luck then, and in case you're interested, I'm the one who started it way back when. There's even a silver cup for the winning dog named after me." She opened the door.

"No, wait! I need your help," he said, bouncing up and down on his heels. He reached in his pocket and pulled out a roll of bills. "I've got money. David's paying me to train Breaker. He made me promise not to steal from my dad anymore."

She held up her hands. "Put your money away." Her eyebrows scrunched into a frown. "Perhaps you've forgotten what I said when you took Breaker. If you want to show him, I won't stop you. Just don't expect me to help."

He looked down and saw the sole of her shoe had come loose. He pushed the money toward her. "I wouldn't be so quick to turn down the cash. You could fix your shoe, for example."

She eyed the offending object indifferently and signaled him to follow her. The flap, flap of the loose sole punctuated their way down the dark hall. To the right, a door opened onto a cheerful living room with overstuffed chairs. Fresh garden flowers in a cobalt blue vase sat on a round coffee table in front of the fireplace. Even a boy whose own room would never appear on the cover of *House Beautiful* knew this room didn't look like her. She continued on, eyes straight ahead, past the dining room with twin mahogany buffets holding matching sets of antique dishes. At the end of the hall, she stopped and took out a key. "My private office. Mona's not permitted."

Benny nodded. That explained the cheerful living room.

She held out an arm and swept Benny inside. A sliver of light snuck through a gap in the floor-length, dark draperies. Old dog show catalogues and yellowed newspaper clippings were strewn everywhere, even under the keyhole desk. On the walls, the flocked wallpaper was barely visible, hidden by what seemed like a hundred old black- and-white photos. A series of younger Besses holding silver trophies and handsome standard poodles with various colored coats stared out from them. It felt kind of creepy, like a horror movie where an old woman who had nothing to live for except faded memories was plotting something ghastly for her handsome young nephew.

He was about to tell her he had to get home and take out the garbage when she snapped on a lamp on a round table next to a wingback chair. She brushed some crumbs that might have come from dog biscuits and sat, motioning him to the opposite chair.

"Is that smell old poodle fur?" he asked, wiggling his nose like a prairie dog popping out of its hole.

She gave him a withering glance, and he shrank into his seat.

"Poodles do not smell," she corrected in a growl scarcely above a whisper. It was a lot more effective than the shouting he'd gotten used to before his parents' divorce. "Poodles don't have fur like other dogs. It's real hair and grows, like yours. Consequently, it doesn't smell, unless the owner never shampoos it." She peered at him with big eyes. "You do shampoo occasionally yourself, I imagine?"

He rubbed his hand over his bangs. They ruffled back down over his forehead like falling dominoes. He would have given anything if his bangs would slick back like his mother's favorite movie star's, or tumble in dark curls over his forehead like David's, but no matter how much goop he squeezed on, they came out like he had shampooed with Vaseline. "Sorry, no offense."

She softened at once. "None taken. You didn't know." She crossed her legs and turned full face to him. "You were saying you wanted my help. I can think of three reasons against it. First, it takes a lot of work to be in a dog show. Second, you don't like poodles, which are the only kind of dog around here — except for Lotus, of course. And third, Breaker isn't settled down enough for you to handle him in the ring."

He grimaced. His plan wasn't working. He thought about bolting, but then he imagined his mother's smile when she saw him holding the blue ribbon and slogged on. "I can work hard when I want to, and I like some poodles. For example, I like McCreery and I like Breaker. If you helped me, I'm sure I could do it."

She shook her head. "It'd never work."

He squirmed in his chair. His favorite TV show was coming on in twenty minutes, and she was wasting his time. He stood, preparing to leave. "All right. If you won't help me with Breaker, I'll take Lotus."

Her next words were softer than he expected. "Lotus is a sweet dog with a cute personality and a pretty little face, but she's not registered with the AKC — the American Kennel Club. You can't enter her in an official dog show."

"No problem," he insisted, waving her objections away with his hand. "A dog doesn't need to be purebred for junior showmanship. David says ..."

He clamped his hand to his mouth, sure he had just lost his last chance, but all she said was, "David's quite the man for all seasons."

"Oh, yes, ma'am. He's a real clever guy. Dr. Kate's crazy about him." He cringed and covered his mouth again.

Her thick eyebrows shot up. "She knows about this idea of yours?"

"It was practically her idea. I mean mine." He blushed. "What I mean is she thinks it'd be fantastic if I had a hobby going to dog shows."

"Really?" she answered absently, as if she weren't really listening. She rose. "I'm hungry. You hungry? Mona made a coconut layer cake."

He flashed a relieved smile. "I'm always hungry. My stepmother doesn't like my baby fat. She has me on a diet." He thrust out his stomach and patted it tenderly.

She rolled her eyes and signaled him to follow her to the kitchen. She grabbed two plates and two forks and placed them and a three-layer cake on the table. "Sit," she invited. She cut two large slices and placed one in front of Benny. "David's favorite," she explained, licking a finger. She sat and took a large bite. A sprinkling of coconut fell onto her shirt, but she didn't notice. She looked across the table, deep into his eyes, as if she wanted to know a part of him that couldn't be seen.

He squirmed uncomfortably. What was she up to? He was the one trying to con her, not the other way around, but that's how it was beginning to feel. "So, anyway, I was hoping you could give me a few pointers," he said, redirecting her to the purpose of his visit. "The Housatonic Dog Show is practically here, so it won't be that much work."

She brushed his words onto the floor along with a few stray crumbs. "Here's what I'll do. I'll teach you about dog shows and handling, but only until Housatonic. After that, you're on your own."

He narrowed his eyes suspiciously. Something didn't feel right. She had something up her sleeve, but what? Still, he was getting what he wanted, wasn't he?

A creaking noise at the door made them both turn to look. A nose appeared through the crack and then a head. McCreery padded softly into the quiet room, his nails clicking on the linoleum. He looked first at one and then the other, as if deciding, and then made a tight circle on the floor between them, measuring the space so as to divide it equally. He sank down with one paw draped gracefully over the other and waited patiently, as if expecting news.

Benny turned to Bess with a guilty look on his face. In his worries about Breaker, he had forgotten all about McCreery. Breaker was his dog now, but McCreery had a special place in his heart and always would. "I think McCreery should come along on Breaker's workouts. He'll be jealous if the puppy gets all the attention. You're too old to run around anymore, and he could use the exercise."

McCreery tossed his head and grinned, so Benny decided he was on the right track.

Bess clasped her hands together and smiled approvingly. "Good idea. No reason for him to sit around getting fat and lazy. Besides, you're right about his jealousy. He's been top dog around here for a long time, and he's not planning to yield to his son any time soon."

Benny scrunched up his nose, considering. He would hate to hurt McCreery's feelings, but he needed Breaker to win at Housatonic. "Can't there be two top dogs?"

"Obviously not," she answered, fluttering her eyelashes.

He decided he would worry about it later. He held up his hand for a high five. "Deal?"

She hesitated, unsure what it meant. Then she remembered something she had seen on TV and slapped back. "Deal!"

Chapter 26

Without Benny, the kitchen seemed empty, like a book without words. Bess sat quietly for a minute, wondering if the boy had outsmarted her somehow. She shook her head. No, that wasn't possible — unless David had.

She heard a noise behind her. She turned, supposing it was McCreery. Instead, her shame-faced twin stepped out of the pantry.

"Eavesdropping again?" Bess asked archly.

Mona attempted a hurt expression and held out a jar of apple butter with "Umpawaug Valley" on the label. "I was hunting for this when you and Benny came in. You know how a person can live without apple butter for months and then all of a sudden gets the hungries for it? Before I could announce my presence, Benny was pouring his heart out and doing a good job of remembering all of David's hints while he was at it. The poor kid would've been flummoxed if I'd popped out from nowhere."

Bess rolled her eyes.

Mona held up a thick piece of rye bread with a questioning look. Bess studied the cake and then the apple butter. She stuck the cake in the fridge. Mona pulled another slice of rye bread out of a white bakery sack and popped both into the toaster.

Bess sat. "For your information, I'm not in the least

deceived by David's transparent ruse to involve me in Breaker's show career. He should be ashamed using the boy like that, but he'll find out the joke is on him."

"You don't say?"

"Strange, I'm not sure the boy likes poodles any more than he used to, but he really wants to be in that dog show. I'm certain of it."

The toaster popped. Mona gave a slice to her sister and sat herself. "Can he win? The boy I mean?"

Bess reached across the table for the apple butter. "Possibly. It's a little country show only worth a point or two — unless Hannah packs it with her dogs — and I'll be teaching him." She screwed up her mouth determinedly and gave the jar a strong twist. "The lid's stuck."

Mona reached behind her and pulled a gadget out of the junk drawer. "Here, I ordered it from a catalogue. Something to help old ladies like us with no men handy for opening jars."

Bess gave a disgusted grunt, but took it anyway. The lid opened on the first twist, and the smell of overripe apples filled the room. She wiped her fingers on the hem of her shirt. "When David sees I can turn my back on a winning dog, he'll have to believe I'm serious. Maybe then he'll stay out of my business."

Mona frowned prettily. "But what about the boy? Won't winning build up his hopes all the more?"

Bess slathered a swath of apple butter across her toast. "Maybe, but maybe he'll be satisfied. He doesn't seem like the type who can stick with anything very long."

Mona reached for the jar. "I have to agree with you there," she said, surprising her sister.

"The best outcome would be for Hannah to take Breaker. A puppy like him deserves a show career. David knows that much, and if he doesn't, Hannah will be sure to inform him."

"You mean, if you can resist a winning puppy?"

"Exactly."

⚜⚜⚜

Sonya placed a frosty martini glass at her husband's elbow. "I thought Benny promised to turn over a new leaf. I had to take out the trash myself three times this week."

Benny's dad kept his eyes on the Red Sox batter. "He's training a puppy for the old lady next door. At least he's stopped whining about getting a dog."

"That's all well and good, but who's going to train Benny? That's what I'd like to know."

"He got an 83 on a math test, and he actually finished his homework every night this week. I checked. If he keeps that up, he and I will be partners yet. Neusner and Neusner, Attorneys at Law."

She grimaced. Her insides felt like a size ten foot trying to squeeze into a size four shoe. Dr. Kate had reminded them both in their meeting last week that Benny's academic horizons were limited, but his father still couldn't face facts. "So you approve of this dog business?" she asked evenly, skirting the issue.

He nodded. "For now, as long as he keeps up his schoolwork. Holding the dogs out as lure may help him stay focused. It's the carrot-and-stick approach coaches use to keep their athletes eligible academically."

"Mmm," she murmured thoughtfully. "And his mother? What about her?"

"If he has another good week, he can see her on her birthday." He picked up the glass and stared into the clear liquid like a fortune teller with a crystal ball. "I only hope she doesn't let the boy down."

CHAPTER 27

Housatonic was a small-time country event compared to Westminster, but to Benny's eyes, it was as confusing as a shopping mall with no signs on the stores. Pedigree dogs of all sizes and shapes were heading toward a large canvas tent, and as far as Breaker was concerned, every one of them looked and smelled delightful. Off to one side, a refreshment stand displayed a blinking neon hot dog slathered with yellow mustard. Benny wished he had one right now to calm his stomach.

David swept his arm in an arc across the campus and announced, "Once upon a time all this was part of the famous Danbury State Fair. Back when Bess and Mona were girls, every school in Connecticut closed on a Friday and kids got in for free."

"Cool," Benny exclaimed, remembering with a shudder the homework piled up and waiting for him at home. Summer school had started last week, and his dad expected him to be stuck in his room every night hitting the books.

They loaded the mountain of paraphernalia a poodle needs to look his best onto a cart and started for the grooming area. Benny gripped Breaker's lead tightly, but so far the puppy had managed the excitement without getting too rambunctious. Four Pekingese on intertwined leads passed nearby, and he didn't let out a peep.

They stopped at a table near the entrance so David could buy a show catalogue. It listed the name of every dog entered, the dog's parents, and the owner. Serious breeders studied it like the bible.

Breaker reverted to his old self as they approached the grooming area. He strained at the lead while Benny stumbled along behind, the sides of his blue blazer flapping like fins. They careened their way down the length of the tent, past more than one handler who raised an eyebrow or snickered at the sorry display.

Benny gulped as he saw Bess waiting in the section where most poodle handlers had set up their gear, her arms crossed in a silent expression of distaste. She grabbed the lead and gave a no-nonsense yank downward. "Sit," she ordered. Like an Olympic obedience champion, Breaker sat. She circled the puppy, studying every inch. When she finished, she handed the lead back to Benny. "Here, try and do likewise."

"Greetings, Mother," David said, bringing up the rear with the cart. He removed his blue blazer, the twin of Benny's, and pointed to the portable grooming table waiting to be set up. "Care to lend a hand?"

She sniffed and turned to Benny. "Good luck, son. Just keep telling yourself, 'I'm in charge,' and you'll do fine." With a cool look at David, she left, presumably to find a seat in the spectators' section.

"Bess still seems mad at you. I thought you two made up," Benny said. He hated when his mother looked at him like that, and it probably didn't feel any better when you were old.

David shrugged indifferently. "I'm not worried. If Breaker makes a good showing today, she'll be hooked."

Benny tried a weak smile. Maybe David was the one fooling himself because he wanted her to be happy so much.

Benny signaled Breaker onto the grooming table. The puppy hopped on board immediately. Grooming is part of a poodle's life, and Breaker was learning. He could be shown in puppy trim today, so the job was easier than in another six months, but even now the judge would be looking for the promise of a full mane. Before Benny was through, Breaker's topknot needed to look and feel like brown velvet fluff. Unfortunately, the puppy decided the shiny metal object was a delightful doggie toy and kept nibbling on the handle. Benny waved a liver treat under his nose. Distracted for the moment, Breaker allowed him to fluff out his tail and ears. The puppy looked so fine Benny spat in his hand and slicked back his own bangs. They were ready to win.

Benny scanned the crowd of handlers and dogs gathering for the various classes. At barely six months of age, Breaker would be shown in the youngest class of puppy dogs. He was pretty certain Hannah wouldn't pass up the chance to show off Chicory, the black puppy that looked so much like Breaker.

Hannah must have been looking for them, too, because her hand shot up and waved them over to the ring where the American Eskimo dogs were finishing up. A stack of crates was piled up beside her. Two of Breaker's sisters were soft-mouth wrestling at the end of Hannah's lead, and a third was waiting in a crate off to one side. A man Benny assumed to be Hannah's handler was putting the final touches on a full-grown male, scissoring his coat, resetting the lines of the trim, and smoothing out the finish. The way the dog stood patiently made the job look easy, but it took years of practice to do it right. Benny could hardly believe that under the fancy haircut, the dog was the same as McCreery and Breaker, but the funny part was the dog didn't look that silly. He had the same winning smile and mischief in his eye as the two poodles Benny had grown to love.

Hannah pulled her glasses down to the end of her nose and stared at Benny like he was a cockroach on a fancy dinner she had paid a lot of money for. "I didn't know you were entering Breaker in junior showmanship," she told David in a thin voice.

The color rose in Benny's cheeks, and David laid a warning hand on his arm. "You remember Benny Neusner," he told Hannah. "He'll be handling Breaker today in the class for six-to-nine-month-old puppy dogs. Bess has been training him herself."

Appeased, Benny leaned down and peered inside the crate at Hannah's feet. "Where's Chicory?"

Hannah shifted uncomfortably. "He got a sliver of glass stuck in his paw last night. Someone broke a soda bottle and failed to clean up properly. The vet said it was only a surface wound but enough to keep him home today."

Benny shuddered, imagining how he would feel if something like that happened to Breaker.

Hannah nodded at a young puppy dog that was waiting patiently for his turn in the ring. "Looks like Breaker will only have one dog to beat in the first class — his brother Licorice."

Benny wrinkled his nose. Had Hannah named all the puppies after food? "Looks like you've got your hands full even without Chicory," he said, pointing at Hannah's three female puppies.

David nodded. "There could be enough for a major."

Benny frowned. "What's that?"

"A major win means defeating a substantial number of the same breed at a single show. The number of dogs needed varies in different sections of the country and from breed to breed," David explained.

Hannah stepped in to clarify. "For a major, it usually takes winning several classes at a single show. Otherwise, there wouldn't be enough dogs to beat. The class between

Breaker and Licorice is only the start."

David nodded. "The really big shows are worth five points. To become a champion and be invited to a show like Westminster, dogs need to earn fifteen points. They have to win two majors, each worth three, four, or five points, and they must win under different judges. The remaining points can come from shows worth any number of points as long as the total adds up to fifteen."

Benny wrinkled his forehead. "It sounds like a lot of work. Wouldn't one major be enough?"

David laughed. "Two are supposed to keep mediocre dogs from accruing enough points from cheap wins against slim competition."

Hannah's smile widened as she readied a surprise. "Chicory's three sisters will be in the same class, and you'll never guess who's offered to help."

Benny and David turned together to look where Hannah was pointing. Bess saw them and waved. Her smile could have lit up a parking lot. She was holding the lead of a graceful black female who, like the others, had grown considerably in the past few months. Breaker had grown, too, but the change didn't seem as dramatic in a puppy they saw every day.

They were interrupted by the sound of someone blowing into a microphone. "Testing, testing," a man's deep voice announced. "Standard poodle males, six to under nine months, in ring three."

"That's you, Benny. The steward will give you a paper with a number to put on your sleeve and show you to your place," Hannah said helpfully. "The judge will signal you to come up for inspection when it's your turn."

Bess had taught Benny that every kind of dog was judged against a standard written by the national organization for that breed. The PCA — the Poodle Club of America — wrote the ones for all three varieties of poodles: toys, miniatures, and standards. The judge picked the dog that came closest to meeting the written standard, or at least he was supposed to. Bess had hinted that someone occasionally picked a particular dog for reasons that had little to do with the standard, but most judges were hardworking, superbly trained experts on many different breeds.

Benny took his place behind Licorice, not that it was much of a line with only the two puppies. Still, this was his first competition — and Breaker's — and once David took his seat at ringside, he was hit with a touch of nerves. He looked around for a friendly face and recognized Licorice's handler as the man he had spotted grooming Hannah's dogs. He was middle-aged, tall and reedy, with black wire-rimmed glasses and kind eyes.

Benny wiped the light sweat blistering his forehead and dried his hand on the side of his pants. "I'm Benny, Benny Neusner," he said, his inexperience sticking out like extra elbows.

The man gave Breaker an admiring once-over and offered Benny his free hand. "Felix Barnet," he said with a buck-toothed grin. He was about to say more when the show steward signaled them both to circle the ring. "Good luck, Benny Neusner," he said kindly.

Benny double wrapped the lead around his hand. "I'm in charge, I'm in charge," he repeated under his breath. He completed the circle and then moved to the side, watching carefully as the judge put Licorice through his paces. The inspection went exactly the way Bess had described, and he felt his confidence growing.

The judge waved Licorice off to the side, and all eyes turned to Benny and Breaker. Benny leaned down and whispered into Breaker's ear, "This is it, boy. Here we go." They stepped up to the judge, and Benny felt the color rise in his cheeks as it occurred to him how embarrassing it would be if they messed up, especially with Bess watching. Fortunately, Breaker got a helpful dose of stage fright himself. He stood calmly for the judge's hands-on inspection and walked sedately down and back without a hitch. The judge ordered both dogs to circle the ring once more. Then he handed Benny the blue ribbon.

Chapter 28

David held up a high five as Benny and Breaker danced out of the ring. Benny slapped back, but his gaze was still on the ribbon. He rubbed his thumb over its silky softness and handed it to David, eyes lingering.

David studied the dark blue silk. "Breaker's first win. Yours, too. How'd you like to have it?"

Benny's eyes widened, but he had been fooled before. "It's not a trick? For keeps?"

An old sadness bubbled up in David and escaped in a sigh. "No trick. For keeps."

If Hannah was upset by Breaker's win, she did a good job of hiding it. Benny only had time to slip the ribbon into his jacket pocket before she was standing in front of him with her hand outstretched. "Congratulations," she said, nodding at David and pumping Benny's hand up and down.

Benny wondered where Bess was. His stomach rumbled, and he remembered he had been too nervous for a real breakfast, just a half dozen jelly donuts and a quart of orange juice. "Maybe Bess is getting herself a hot dog," he said. "A couple of footlongs with double chili cheese and sauerkraut would taste good about now. And a slice of pepperoni pizza if they have any."

Hannah and David rolled their eyes and smiled. "I'll

go," David offered.

Hannah studied Benny with new interest. "You'll have a bit of a wait before you and Breaker go up against the other winners. All the other male poodles need to compete in their classes first."

Benny glanced at the ring where Felix was waiting to take in the black dog in full coat he had seen earlier. The big dog pranced in place like a thoroughbred racehorse at the starting gate. "Him, too?" he gulped.

"If he wins his class."

"And that's it?"

She shook her head. "Not really. The whole routine is repeated for the females. Winners Dog and Winners Bitch compete for Best of Breed. Jim and Holly Wren have brought their champion DandyBoy. He'll be hard to beat."

"And that's it?" he squeaked. He was tired just thinking about it.

She laughed her deep rumbly laugh. "I'm afraid not. The winners of each breed in the Group compete against each other. Poodles are in a Group called Non-Sporting."

"You mean poodles have to compete against dogs like Dalmatians and bulldogs?"

"All the winning Non-Sporting dogs go up against each other. They are judged against their own standard. If a bulldog's wrinkles or a Dalmatian's spots fall short, some other breed will win. Sometimes it seems like Non-Sporting is where they put all the dogs that don't fit someplace else — except toy poodles compete in the Toy Group. It's a little confusing at first."

He bobbed his head vigorously. "I'll say. And that's it?"

"Just one more. The seven Group winners go up against each other, and that winner is Best in Show."

He sighed. "It sure is a lot of work."

She made her excuses and left Benny to himself. His mouth was watering for those hot dogs, and he wondered where David had disappeared.

The announcer called for bred-by-exhibitor male dogs. Jim Wren was at the head of the line holding the lead of a beautiful black dog. Benny hadn't seen Jim earlier and decided he and Holly must have arrived late. The dogs went through their paces, and Jim's won easily. Jim stuck the ribbon in his pocket and looked around.

"Over here," Benny called from the sidelines where he was still waiting for his snack. "Congratulations," he said, shaking Jim's hand.

Jim looked proudly at the beautiful dog sitting quietly but alert by his side. "Yes, DandyBoy is having a good day. We're hoping to finish his championship today. Then we'll enter him in specials and build up his record. Plenty of stud fees for a dog with a big record."

Benny had been gossiping too long, and Breaker was tired of it. The puppy preferred to become better acquainted with DandyBoy and tried nosing under his tail. "Oooh, that's gross," Benny said, yanking Breaker back. He spotted David heading toward them with a white cardboard box. Breaker saw him, too, and broke free of his lead. He landed on David's chest with his two front paws. David barely saved Benny's lunch.

Jim hid a smile and excused himself to search for his wife.

"Do you think it was a good idea to let Breaker get the upper hand just now?" David asked, wiping a glob of chili cheese off his cheek with a paper napkin. "What happened to 'I'm in charge'?"

Benny looked around guiltily, hoping Bess hadn't noticed his slip-up. "I bet Bess is in the ladies' room crying over how much she wishes she'd taken Breaker in herself." He was kidding, but from what he had smelled of the portable toilets, she wouldn't be spending a lot of time in there. He scanned the people at ringside and saw her rise from her seat. She picked the show catalogue off the empty seat beside her and stuck it in her purse, apparently preparing to leave. Breaker still had several more classes to go.

"Wait!" he called, but she was too far away to hear. He started after her, hot dog in hand. She got as far as the edge of the parking lot before she turned and headed back to the spectators' section. He smiled knowingly. The contest of wills between David and her wasn't over yet.

Two chili cheese hot dogs, an ice cream sandwich and a strawberry milkshake later, all the male standard poodle classes were finished, and it was time to choose the best of them. Breaker, Black Bean, and DandyBoy lined up with the other class winners.

The judge walked down the line and looked them over with obvious pleasure. When it was Breaker's turn to be called out, he stood calmly as the judge determined that his bones and muscles were as they should be; but when the judge examined his bite, the puppy did a soft-mouth nibble on the judge's hand. In the front row at ringside, Bess couldn't help smiling. McCreery had done the same at his age.

The judge pulled out a white handkerchief and wiped his fingers. "Take him down to the end and back."

"I'm in charge. I'm in charge," Benny repeated under his breath as Breaker took off at full gallop. Benny was supposed to match his pace perfectly to the dog's, but he failed to keep up. Feet flying, he trailed along behind until he arrived at the end of the ring a full lead behind Breaker. Miraculously, Breaker stood quietly at attention like he was supposed to, waiting for the command to return.

Benny straightened his tie and took a deep breath. He gave the signal to move forward, but instead of trotting back down the ring to where the judge was tapping his foot impatiently, Breaker yanked the lead from his hand

and leaped high into the air. The crowd gasped, as much at the height of his spring as at his impertinence. Benny reached into his pocket for a liver treat. Breaker grabbed for it, nearly bowling him over. In the split second it took Breaker to swallow, Benny regained the lead. He looked around anxiously, uncertain what to do.

The judge motioned with one finger for him to come back to the start. This time Breaker obeyed. The tall judge leaned down and whispered in his ear, "I'm going to forget what I just saw. Now, try again."

Benny held the lead firmly and shook his finger sternly at the grinning puppy. "You heard the judge. No more fooling around." Breaker shook his coat back into place and pawed the ground eagerly. Benny gave the signal and off they went.

From her seat in the stands, Bess could tell something special was happening. She had experienced it only a few times in her life at the end of the lead. Every muscle in Breaker's body extruded an almost palpable electricity that lit up the ring like flashing cameras pursuing a Hollywood starlet. It was as if generations of champion Umpawaug poodles had come to life in that one dog. Breaker was doing what he was born to do and loving every minute. The crowd felt it, too. A ripple of applause broke out at ringside as he and Benny made their final turn and came to a stop at the end of the line. The judge gave Breaker a final look and called out Black Bean. It was time to wait again.

The judge moved quickly through the remaining dogs. When he was finished, he walked slowly down the line, hands behind his back. He nodded to one, two, three dogs, telling them to step forward. Black Bean and DandyBoy were among them. Motioning with his hand, he told Benny to stand in front of Jim in the short line.

Benny was pretty sure Breaker was in the line for the finalists. His whole body tingled with excitement, and he had to fight to keep himself still. He could tell Breaker was feeling the same. The judge spun on his heel and faced the remaining dogs. "Thank you," he said and signaled they were excused.

In the stands, Bess held her breath, a half-eaten sandwich forgotten on the seat beside her. A fly buzzed around it unnoticed.

The judge walked slowly down the short line, studying the four dogs carefully. When he stopped in front of Breaker, Benny's heart beat faster. What if he asked him to go around the ring again, so people could get one last look? Who knew what Breaker would do given another chance, now, when the end was so near?

The judge walked back to the head of the line. He opened his mouth, started to ask the dogs to circle once more and thought better of it.

Benny squeezed his eyes shut and wished with all his might. He opened them when he felt someone standing close in front of him.

The judge leaned over and whispered in his ear. "That was the worst display I've seen in all my years of judging. Try to do better next time." Then he handed him a small silver bowl. Breaker stuck his nose inside, curious whether there was something good for the winning dog to eat, and gave a disappointed sniff. It wasn't exactly Winners Dog manners, but Benny was too preoccupied to care. Hot prickles behind his eyelids threatened to turn into tears as he rubbed his fingers gently across the trophy's engraving: "The Bess Rutledge Trophy — Winners Dog."

Amid the polite applause, David edged through the crowd to where Benny and Breaker were waiting for the show photographer. He swiveled his head in all directions, scanning the crowd for Bess. Their eyes met and held. She tucked her purse under her arm and left.

Chapter 29

Benny was in a rush to get home and polish the silver trophy named in Bess's honor. His mother's birthday was tomorrow, and he wanted it to shine like new. He had almost reached the gate when he spotted Steffie sitting on the long bench.

"Whoa!" he said with his mouth hanging open. She was smearing on some black lipstick she must have kept hidden in her backpack all day. The color matched the black smudges under her eyes. Two tufts of orange hair stuck out from each side of her head like horns. Her red hightops were the only part of her outfit that wasn't black. "You going Gothic on me?" he asked, disappointed his little flower child was gone. "Not that you don't look totally cool."

"It's because we Aspies don't know how to interact appropriately in social situations," she said.

Benny's gaze went to her nose.

"It's not a real stud if that's what you're wondering. I used Elmer's on a brass do-dad I found in my dad's toolbox. It'll come off, I think." She shifted so she could see him better. "So how are things going with Dr. Kate and that friend of yours, David?"

He shrugged. "Not so hot, but I can fix that. My dad had a late meeting with a client last night, and Sonya and I watched one of her chick flicks. A boy convinced his mom a certain guy was in love with her, and sure enough, they got married. Her first husband got killed in a horrible train wreck, so it worked out okay. I picked up some really cool tips."

She slipped the lipstick into her backpack. "I hope you're right. Love can be tough on a person."

His heart gave a little flutter. He had seen her and Adam yesterday with their heads bent over a thick calculus book. Adam had said something, and Steffie stared up at him with a goofy-looking smile like she understood what he was talking about.

Benny gathered up his courage. "I saw you and Adam yesterday," he said unable to smother a little pout.

"Yeah, Adam's cool, but he's just a friend. Nothing serious."

He swallowed hard. It hadn't occurred to him things could have gone as far as she said they hadn't. "Sometimes I think I must be an Aspie myself. I've decided I like dogs better than people, at least some of them."

"Good point. Dogs are cool."

"I think Bess might be an Aspie, too. Can old people get it?"

"Depends," she answered noncommittally. She reached into the bowels of her backpack and fished out some nail polish. She held it up to the light. "It's supposed to be black, but I think I goofed." She checked the label and shrugged. "Oh, well, my mother'll still flip out over Midnight Blue." She swiped the brush across her thumb nail and blew. "So, any news?"

"You mean about the pizza party Friday for everyone who does their homework all week?"

She pulled a face. "Hardly. Did you tell Dr. Kate about 'you know what'?"

He stuck out his chin defensively. "Maybe."

She swiped a blue streak down the middle of her thumb nail like she was more interested in that than him, but he could tell she was upset. "I saw a program on TV where a kid our age got put in jail for having drugs in school," she said. She sliced an index finger across her throat like a knife and stuck out her tongue. With the black lipstick circling her mouth, she looked like Morticia.

He gulped.

"Don't worry. If that happens to you, I'll bake you a cake with a file in it."

He leaped to his feet, his hands balled into fists. "Ha, ha! Very funny. I suppose you'll blame it on being an Aspie, but it sucked." He shrugged into his backpack and headed toward Gallows Hill Road, pumping his legs harder than he ever had before in his life.

"Just kidding," she called after him, her voice cracking.

He didn't answer. His head was spinning. For the first time in his life, he had found a school where he felt safe and a girl who was his best friend, or at least she used to be. What if they both were slipping through his fingers, and all because of a secret he couldn't tell even her?

Chapter 30

Benny headed downstairs from Dr. Kate's office, shoulders sagging and eyes on his feet. The silver cup dangled carelessly from one finger. He watched it slide onto the floor, rocking back and forth like an empty carriage on a Ferris wheel. His mother didn't care about the stupid cup, and neither did he. She never even bothered to see it.

"Mind if we sit?"

Benny jumped. He was so caught up in his misery he hadn't noticed David and Breaker joining him. Breaker's puffy tail waved back and forth like a hummingbird. Benny tried to ignore him, but the puppy nudged his arm with his nose like a sheepdog herding a lamb. Benny pulled the puppy closer, as if David might snatch him away.

"A dog can be a great pal," David said.

"Better than some people," Benny muttered under his breath.

David had a pretty good idea about Benny's problem. Dr. Kate had surprised him with a phone call this morning. She only wanted to talk about Benny, not his dinner invitation, but he was pleased anyway. Maybe she was beginning to trust him with the boy.

"Dr. Kate told me about your mother's birthday. She heard about it from your teacher, so it wasn't private. I know you were looking forward to spending the day with her."

Benny scooped up a pebble and heaved it across the lawn. His voice dropped to a whisper. "It was supposed to be our time. She promised."

The boy's pain stirred David's own youthful memories, but his job now was to help the boy move on from his disappointment. "I'm sorry," he said, "but you can't go on licking your wounds forever. You've got to get back up on the horse and ride."

Benny stood, his jaw clenched. "You calling my mother a horse?"

"What I mean," David said, measuring his words like a thrifty housewife, "is nothing takes your mind off troubles like plunging back into work. A dog show my mother never misses is coming up. We could take Breaker."

Benny jutted his neck out like an angry turtle. "You're kidding, right? Breaker doesn't want to be in any stupid dog show, do you, boy?"

The puppy sniffed his face with a worried frown.

David took a deep breath. He didn't want to lose the boy now. He had seen Bess's expression when the judge handed Breaker the trophy at Housatonic. His heart used to twist into jealous knots when her face lit up over a dog. Now he would give anything to see it again.

"Can you believe it?" he asked, putting all the enthusiasm he could muster into his voice. "Breaker winning a five-point major at six months? Even I never expected him to beat DandyBoy. If that doesn't bring Bess to her senses, nothing will."

Benny stepped off the porch and kicked the grass. Sonya would kill him for scuffing up his good lace shoes, but he didn't care. "Good for you, but it's not my problem. Bess is your mother, not mine, and mine doesn't give a damn what I do."

David stood, too. He wished Kate were here to help. He tried to remember what would have worked for him at Benny's age. He picked the silver cup up off the floor and traced the words with his finger. "I know how you feel. When I was a kid, I wasn't crazy about dogs, but I faked it. Once, I insisted Bess let me enter junior showmanship even though I knew I'd hate every minute of it." He lowered his voice confidentially. "I wanted her to love me."

Benny stared like David had just shed an invisibility cloak. He squeezed his hands into tight fists. If Dr. Kate had been there, she would have said he was fighting his emotions, rushing to do the very thing that would cause him pain. "I'm giving Breaker back to Bess. She's only pretending he belongs to me anyway."

David caught him by the elbow before he could bolt. "She won't keep him. She'll hand him over to Hannah." He brought his face in close, locking Benny's eyes. "You can't make a person love someone, not even a dog. You should have figured that out by now."

The muscles around Benny's mouth twitched like over-tightened rubber bands. David froze in place as his words came back to him with a meaning he hadn't intended. Man and boy stared at each other as in a mirror.

David broke first. "That didn't come out right. I didn't mean it the way it sounded."

Benny looked away. He picked up the silver cup. "Come on, Breaker," he said, signaling the puppy to follow. "Sorry, David," he called back over his shoulder. "Sorry, sorry."

Chapter 31

The knock on the door caught Bess unawares. Mona was out, and she wasn't expecting anyone herself. Whoever it was, McCreery's ears twitched, but he stayed in his dog nest, his chin resting comfortably on his toy fish. Bess pulled back the kitchen curtain. It was the boy, holding the silver cup and looking around nervously in the gathering dusk. Breaker was sitting beside him, calm for once. She considered pretending she wasn't home. She hadn't completely recovered from Housatonic. The last thing she wanted tonight was a debate with one of David's emissaries. Still, she could handle a mere boy.

"Well?" she asked, opening the door. Benny seemed to have grown. Even though he stood on the step below, he towered over her.

He thrust the silver cup at her. "Here. It's got your name on it."

She took the cup and turned it slowly in her hands, enjoying the cool, smooth feel of it. When she was done, she handed it back. She never even glanced at the puppy.

Benny stuck his toe in the door before she could close it. "Wait, the cup's yours for keeps. Breaker, too. He's your dog no matter what you pretend. My dad won't let him in the house. And by the way, I think you should know David wants me to keep on being his handler."

"What did you tell him?"

He stuck out his lower lip. "I told him it's between you and him. I've got my own problems."

She narrowed her eyes, as if for once she didn't think her son was behind this. "You and Breaker beat some pretty good dogs and their handlers at Housatonic. I'd have thought you'd be eager to get back into the ring."

He shifted uncomfortably, a fish in a net. "What for? I only did it for my mother, hoping she'd be proud of me. You know, like David did when he was little. Well, she couldn't care less, any more than you did."

Her mouth dropped open. "David? What are you talking about?"

He had been scared by that look before, but he was determined to finish what he had come to say. "You know. Pretending he cared about your stupid dog shows so you'd pay attention to him. It was dumb, but he couldn't think of anything better. He was only a kid." He waited, leg jiggling. If Bess was anything like his mother, he was in big trouble.

She braced herself against the doorjamb, swinging her head back and forth like a loose gate in the wind. "No, you're wrong."

Breaker pulled free and put his paws on her shoulders, sniffing her face with a worried frown like McCreery had done a hundred times before.

Benny tipped back his head and made a loud guffaw that echoed through the damp twilight. "You don't know much, do you? David's still doing it, for crying out loud. Trust me, he doesn't care about Breaker's show career for his own self, and he definitely doesn't mean for you to leave the poor dog out in the puppy shed and pretend he's not there."

The sound of an approaching car intruded, and they both turned to look. Benny grabbed Breaker's collar, but the puppy was content to watch. Mona climbed out, loaded down with two brown grocery bags. She stopped in her tracks when she saw the three of them in the doorway. She looked the scene over briefly, then continued up the walk without a word. First Benny, then Bess stepped aside so she could pass. Mona turned and looked up at the sky. The evening star was visible through the trees. She held the door open. "It's late and it's cold. You'd better come inside."

Bess studied the puppy for a long moment without a word. Then she proceeded into the house, Breaker dashing in first.

Benny turned and started to leave, but he felt someone watching and looked back over his shoulder. Mona was standing in the lighted doorway, and, unmistakably, she winked at him like they were partners in a conspiracy. Well, maybe they were. Everyone had gotten what they wanted, hadn't they? Breaker would live in a house and have one more person to love him — two counting Mona. David would be happy because his mother wouldn't be all depressed any more. For himself, he was out of dog shows for good, just like he wanted. Everything was terrific. So why wasn't he feeling so hot?

Chapter 32

Benny headed for the school office, carrying the attendance sheet in one hand and tossing M&Ms into his mouth with the other. Now that he wasn't wasting every afternoon trying to teach Breaker some manners, he had plenty of time to think up new hobbies — like this one. He had the best luck with the red ones, not that any went to waste. A little dirt never hurt anyone. In fact, he was so busy with his new life he hardly had a minute to miss Breaker.

Fortunately, Breaker wasn't the only one he was too busy to miss. He could never forgive his former friend Steffie for treating him practically like a criminal. The next time he saw her, he planned to give her the cold shoulder, but when he spotted her sashaying toward him, he forgot. He had never seen anyone quite like her before, at least not a girl he knew. She was wearing Capri pants that looked like painted-on yellow skin. It was a mystery how she had gotten them over her knees. They rode low on her hips, and her skinny, red tank top was kind of short so he could see the jewel stuck in her navel. He hoped it was like the nose stud and the glue would wear off.

He gulped. "Wow! Did Dr. Kate see you looking like that?" He tried to keep his eyes off the soft bulges sticking out of the tank top, but he couldn't help himself.

Steffie shrugged and hooked a finger under a spaghetti

strap. "I'm sorry I upset you the other day." She tugged the hem of her tank top. "I always get crabby at my time of the month."

His cheeks burned. At least she hadn't tried to blame it on the List.

She nodded at the garden chairs at the edge of the flower garden. "Got a minute to sit? I finished my test early and am on kind of a break."

He looked down at the attendance sheet and nodded.

She moved her chair so it was touching Benny's. He rested his hand casually on the arm. She did the same, leaving a tiny space between them. There was an awkward pause, and then he asked, "So, where'd you get the new clothes?"

"One of my mom's New York shopping sprees. She's on a kick to get me a boyfriend." She pointed at his new red hightops. "You look cool yourself."

He leaned down, wiping a little smudge off the toe of his shoe. "I bought my new hightops myself," he said. "I'm going to keep my own money from now on after what happened on my mother's birthday."

She touched his arm. "Sorry, Adam told me. Maybe next year."

His arm felt all tingly where she had touched him. He rubbed the spot, not sure if he was trying to wipe it away or make it last. "Yeah, maybe."

She crossed her legs and dangled a strappy shoe off the end of her painted toes. "My mom'll try anything to make me popular. She thinks a boyfriend will cure my Asperger's. She even hinted it'd be all right if I had sex."

His eyes bugged out. "Really? You sure?"

She gave him a sly look. "Pretty sure, but it could be my Asperger's getting me mixed up again."

"I wish my mom thought sex would cure me. She'd be happy if I was a baby all my life. I don't think you should tell

Dr. Kate about the sex part though."

"She wouldn't care. She's a Freudian. They all believe in sex and stuff like that."

He shook his head. "I wouldn't count on it. You can ask her yourself. She's always telling me thinking's okay, but doing's different." He considered a minute. "Exactly how's your mother going to find someone for you to have sex with? I'd be happy to help."

"Ballroom dancing. Miss Bolyne's dance class."

He didn't see what good that would be. "I think I've heard of it."

"Three nights a week. I have to miss *Cosby* and *America's Funniest Home Videos.*"

He felt sorry for her. He wasn't prepared to give up his favorite TV shows for a lame dance class, not even for sex.

She grabbed onto a strand of hair that had come loose from her up-do and twirled it around her finger. It reminded him of a travel movie his teacher had shown about Greece and old men who played with their worry beads. He wondered what Steffie had to worry about.

She started to speak, stopped, drew in a deep breath, and started again. "Try not to get mad, but you really need to listen. Drugs are bad for you, and can get you in a lot of trouble if you're caught."

He got to his feet, his fists curled into balls. "I'm warning you, Steffie."

"What if your dad finds out? He'll yank you out of school, and I'll never see you again."

He gulped. He hadn't thought about that. Nobody had ever cared enough to think about him before. She deserved to know the truth, but she interrupted before he could get it out.

"Getting kicked out would be the dumbest thing you ever did, so try not to be stupid."

His eyes narrowed. In the old days, he would have

punched her one for an insult like that. "Stupid, am I? Well, I'm not so dumb I can't see you're not my friend." He tapped the side of his face and faked surprise. "Oh, wait. The List says you can't make friends, so I guess stupid me is wrong again."

"Then you'll be happy to hear my news," she snapped back. "My parents are taking me to Europe for the whole summer, maybe longer, so you won't have to put up with me anymore."

His mouth dropped open, but no words came out. He turned and ran as fast as he could, his backpack slapping against his spine like he was punishing himself.

She wiped the back of her hand across her nose and sniffed. The tears would make her mascara run, but it didn't matter. She had just lost the best friend she ever had, and all because she cared.

Chapter 33

Benny had given up dogs for good, but he decided he might as well drop by Bess's for old times' sake. Sonya had left a frozen soy burger for dinner, and Mona could be fixing some of her scrumptious meatloaf and mashed potatoes. He'd probably get invited.

He found Bess under a tree, leaning over a metal washtub. Inside, Breaker stood half-covered in suds, head hanging, tangled ears dripping. A ripe odor rose from his wet coat. Benny slapped a copy of the *NHS Gazette* over his nose. He had brought a copy of the school paper so she could read his article about Breaker's big win. He hated to write essays for English class, but a newspaper story was different.

He staggered back, rotating his arms like a windmill. "P.U. What's that stink?"

"Skunk," she answered matter-of-factly. "Breaker's been trying to catch it for days. He got a little too close this time." She dipped a sponge and slopped more suds across Breaker's back.

Benny peeked under the grooming table where McCreery was resting with a smug look on his face. "For once McCreery seems happy that Breaker's getting all the attention," he said with a grin.

The old dog got to his feet, let Benny give him a pat,

and slunk off before Bess could stick him in the tub, too.

"I see you," she called but didn't order him back. She'd had enough of his holier-than-thou attitude for one afternoon.

Benny turned his attention back to Breaker. A rivulet of shampoo rolled down between the puppy's eyes and slid off the end of his nose. "He sure looks skinny with his coat matted down like that."

She nodded at an open can of tomato juice. "Pass me that," she ordered sharply.

He handed it over. "I never knew skunks stank this bad. I'll be smelling it in my dreams, or should I say nightmares?"

She poured the tomato juice over Breaker's head and down his back. He shivered from head to toe, mostly from humiliation, and his bobbed tail resembled a flag in surrender.

Benny poured another can of the red liquid and watched it roll off Breaker's back into the murky water. He sniffed and wrinkled his nose. "Does that stuff really work?" He turned over the can and studied the label to see if "cure for skunk stink" was listed as a recommended use.

"It better. If it doesn't, I'll have to cut him down."

"Cut him down?" he squeaked, shielding his crotch.

"Oh, for heaven's sake," she snapped. "Shave his coat."

He unclasped his hands. "I knew that." He studied her face. Her short gray curls formed a topknot that looked pretty much like Breaker's before the skunk encounter. "Seriously, Bess, who ever dreamed up those crazy poodle hairdos?"

She launched into the speech she had given hundreds of times. "The clip is a tribute to their days as hunters. Poodles are bird dogs, bred originally to retrieve ducks in the icy waters of Northern Europe — probably Germany or Russia. No one's sure."

"So French poodles aren't really French?"

"'French' refers to the cut invented by the French. It's a tribute to their days as bird dogs, really. The puffy chest kept the dog's vital organs warm, and the bracelets on the joints were for the same reason. The hind end was shaved so it wouldn't sink down and pull the dog under."

He studied the puppy with new eyes. With his wet coat matted down against his skin, he looked pretty much like any other hunting dog. He handed her the last tomato juice can. "So chasing skunks is in Breaker's genes?"

"Birds, not skunks." She sniffed cautiously. "Better, but not good enough. We'll have to do the whole thing all over again tomorrow."

"We?" Benny squeaked. "I think I'm supposed to mow the lawn. We like the place to look nice."

She peered at Benny over her glasses, thick eyebrows drawn together. "You should be doing this yourself. He's still half yours."

He shook his head. "If that's what you wanted to tell me, thanks anyway. I've given up trying to impress my mother." He gave Breaker a pat. "I'd better be going. I've got a lot of important stuff on my agenda today." It was one of his mother's favorite expressions.

She wiped stray suds off her cheek with the back of her hand. "Hold on! I thought you wanted me to get back into dogs."

"Not me. David. Like I said, he wants you to be happy."

She dropped the sponge into the tub and rested against the table. "I know. I finally get it. But what about you and your mother?"

He reddened and scuffed the dirt with the toe of his shoe. "It's hopeless."

"Don't be so sure. I'm here to help. From now on, you have my full support." She gave him her most brilliant smile. "How does six a.m. tomorrow sound?"

He bugged out his eyes and bobbed his neck like a

flamingo. Was the woman serious? Hadn't she heard a word he had said? Maybe she was getting deaf. Old people did sometimes. She was right to begin with. He was too young and she was too old to be messing around with dogs. So what if Breaker had been a superstar at Housatonic? What good did that do him? He was about to tell her so when he noticed her face, all smiley and hopeful. If he let her down now, she'd get depressed again and who would David blame? Him! It wasn't fair. It really wasn't. Maybe he could trick her into picking someone else to help her — maybe even David.

He changed his frown to a grin and said, "Dog shows are too much work for a boy like me. I've already got lots to do. For example, I should be home cleaning up my room. Cleanliness is next to godliness, I always say. And I've been thinking about asking my teacher for more homework."

She smiled innocently. "Very sensible. You and Breaker made a great team at Housatonic, but that was just a one-shot deal, a thing of the past. I understand."

He exhaled a huge sigh of relief. That went better than expected. He decided to hang around a bit longer. Old people liked someone to listen to them.

She refilled the tub with fresh water and squirted in shampoo from a bottle with her own handwritten label. She dipped a brush and resumed scrubbing. "Even if the smell goes away, I may have to cancel Breaker's appearance at Quinnipiac next month. No handler."

"Quinnipiac? Sounds foreign."

"It's an Indian tribe that used to live not too far from here. Now it's the name of the biggest dog club in New England, besides Boston. Actually, I used to be the president."

"Well, I hope you find someone to help you, but I feel sorry for Breaker — having to wear that sissy hairdo and all."

"Feel sorry all you want. The dogs love it: standing

alone in the winner's circle, the crowd roaring, cameras flashing."

His eyes grew round. "Cameras? Do they have TV so everyone can see you, even people who can't come because they're too busy?"

"Sure. CNN, Animal Planet — at least at the really top shows." She waited a minute to let the lure of TV fame really settle in. A show big enough for national television could be years away for Breaker — if ever — but this was no time to burst the boy's bubble.

He thought it over, imagining how impressed his mother would be. "Say, when is this Quinnipiac, anyway?"

"A couple of weeks. Fourth of July weekend, actually. Plenty of time if we work hard." She doused Breaker with fresh water and asked Benny, "Toss me that towel, will you?" It was the distraction Breaker had been waiting for. As she raised her hand to catch it, he leaped free of the tub, spraying water where he landed.

"Come back here," she scolded, wiping the spray off her face. She may as well have been ordering the wind. He stuck his hind end up in the air, tail wagging, and dashed back and forth in front of her. Her fingertips barely skimmed his coat as he passed. He came closer, teasing. She lunged and her feet flew out from under her. The puppy froze in place.

Benny rushed over and knelt beside her. He had never seen an old person this helpless before, and it scared him. "Are you all right, Bess?"

She raised up on one elbow and then to a sitting position, wiggling fingers and toes in turn. "No broken bones," she pronounced.

At the sound of her voice, Breaker moved closer and sniffed the back of her hand. She shuddered, like she was remembering a different fall.

She held both arms out to Benny. "Give me a boost."

He grasped her hands and eased her up. She stood, testing her weight. She took a careful step forward, then another. "See, I'm fine."

She called Breaker over to her and gave him a pat. Then she signaled Benny to empty the heavy tub. He dumped the water onto the bare spot where the grass had worn down from the long hours she had spent grooming dogs there over the years. They both watched the water slide in rivulets over the hard dirt and disappear.

She turned and locked eyes with Benny. "Listen, Benny, I've given a lot of thought to what you said the other night about how I've treated my son. I've loved my dogs, and that's not bad, but I've put them above the people who loved me, especially David. How he learned to be kind, I don't know. Probably from my sister Mona."

He started to speak, but she held up a hand for silence and continued. "I'm not going to lie to you. I'm seventy years old. I've been selfish all my life, but I like to think I can change."

Again, he tried to interrupt, but she was too quick.

"I'm not going to pretend I can change completely. I won't always do the right thing, but I do promise to try. I want one last chance at Westminster and I need your help, but I'm not just thinking about me. You'll get what you want, too. If a Westminster win doesn't get your mother's attention, nothing will. So, what do you say? Can we be partners: Rutledge and Neusner?"

He waited, testing whether this time she was finished. He decided she was. He drummed the side of his cheek with his fingers like he was trying to decide. Really, there wasn't that much to think about it. Like Dr. Kate said, some people never change, but maybe Bess could. What she said made sense. They would both get what they wanted. He burst into a grin. "You mean Neusner and Rutledge."

She stuck out a hand. They shook and looked away

awkwardly, uncertain what came next in their new partnership.

"By the way," he said, his face brightening with inspiration, "my parents are going out tonight. Sonya left me a frozen dinner — Vegetable Tofu Surprise — but I ate a big lunch. I can bring it over, and we can share if you're hungry."

She laughed her croupy laugh. "Thanks, anyway. Mona's is making fried chicken with mashed potatoes and gravy. You're invited if you want."

He coughed to cover the sound of his tummy rumbling. "I think I can make it."

She still had something to say and looked Benny in the eye. "I can teach you everything you need to know about being a handler, but dogs can tell how a person feels about them. Breaker is handsome enough to do some winning no matter who takes him into the ring, but unless he has a special bond with his handler, he won't win at the really big shows. Some dogs want to win for their own sakes, but for Umpawaug poodles, their connection with the person on the other end of the lead is what counts. It's made for some seemingly impossible wins."

His face turned red like a schoolboy with his first crush. "No problem. Breaker's my friend now." The puppy pranced over to him and placed two muddy front paws on his white shirt. They grinned at each other until Benny took a dog biscuit out of his pocket and tossed it for Breaker to chase.

A horn honked nearby. Benny jerked up his head, face alight. He still hadn't forgiven his mother for her birthday, but something inside him couldn't help hoping.

"My mom! Wait 'til she hears I'm gonna be on TV." He grabbed his backpack, not bothering to slip it on, and dashed for the stone wall fence. "Tell Mona I'll come another night," he shouted over his shoulder. He swung one leg over the top. The other leg was still stranded on the other side when he halted abruptly, shoulders slumping. "My mistake," he said, pasting on a fake smile. "Maybe tomorrow. I'll tell her the news tomorrow."

Bess felt a lump growing at the base of her throat. Was this how it had been for David all those years ago, waiting for her to come home? She thought of the promise she had just made to Benny and remembered all the promises she had made — and broken — to her son David. She hadn't mentioned Westminster, but she knew Benny was thinking about it. How many times had she tried and disappointed herself at the last minute? Would it happen again, another broken promise to another boy? She pulled her arms tighter across her chest, as if locking the promise inside. Maybe this time would be different. She would try.

Chapter 34

For the first time in months, Mona was greeted by the aroma of fresh coffee she hadn't made herself. The dinner table was set for three, and pink and white impatiens were arranged in a Newcomb pottery vase she recognized from childhood. Most surprising of all, Bess was dressed for the occasion in black pants fresh from the dry cleaners and a red pullover that matched her lipstick

Mona stood back, hands on hips. "Are you going to tell me what you're up to, or do I have to guess?"

Bess rearranged one of the flowers. "I invited Benny for dinner. He and I have reached an understanding about Breaker, a kind of partnership. No big deal."

Mona hid a smile. "Glad to hear it. Now maybe life can get back to normal around here."

Bess jerked her head up. "You aren't planning to leave, are you? Didn't you say the cabinets in your condo aren't finished?" She coughed, hoping to disguise her worry.

Mona sat. "That's right. Actually, I'm taking a little trip to Boca Raton to see for myself how things are progressing. Care to come? We'll be back by the first of August."

Bess sat, too, her face thoughtful. Once Quinnipiac was behind them, Breaker's shows would be over for a while. She could take McCreery with them, and David and Benny could manage Breaker. "I thought you'd be glad to get away from me."

Mona gave a sly smile. "And here I thought you hoped to get rid of me."

Bess crossed her arms. "Oh, for heaven's sake. I'll never understand you if I live to be a hundred."

"I plan to, so you might as well, too. It'll give us both time to figure things out."

Bess tilted her head for a better view of her twin. "I've been thinking I might take a drive over to Woodbridge one day soon. The pasture we played in as kids probably has been bulldozed by a developer, but back in the day, it seemed like heaven to me — the little trail, the black-eyed Susans growing on either side."

"Our special place," the sisters caroled in unison. They peeked at each other out of the corners of their eyes and looked away quickly.

Bess held up a gardening catalog for Mona's inspection. "I'm going to order myself some pink japonica for out front, and I think I'll get some of those old-fashioned roses to go along the back where the kennels used to be. Growing a garden is kind of like raising poodles, don't you think?"

Mona drew in her chin, straightening her back. "I think you're nuts. That's what I think."

Bess tucked the catalogue under her arm and swung her legs around. "I might have expected you to say something like that. For your information, that new clerk at Myers' Pharmacy asked me the other day if we were related. He said I reminded him of you."

Mona sniffed. "Really? For your information, that happens to me all the time. Personally, I don't see the resemblance. Do you?"

Bess shook her head. "Definitely not, but it wouldn't hurt to look."

The twin sisters hoisted themselves up and walked to the antique bull's eye mirror hanging at the end of Bess's front hall. The glass was small and the gilt frame was hung high, so they had to stand close together and stretch their necks upward to include both faces in the round opening.

And that's how McCreery found them when he came downstairs from his afternoon nap. He didn't interrupt, but he couldn't help wondering how long those two old fools were going to stand there, trying to decipher the obvious, before someone remembered to feed the dog.

Chapter 35

McCreery's jealous eyes burned into the back of Bess's neck as she pulled the station wagon out of the driveway, but he would have to get over it. She had her hands full with Benny and Breaker. Quinnipiac wasn't Westminster, but it was the most important show in New England this holiday weekend. Half the cars racing past them were heading for a day's outing at Lake Candlewood; the other half sported bumper stickers saying "Show Dogs on Board" or lettering on the sides to announce a kennel's name. Sometimes small crates with dogs were stacked so high their faces showed through the rear window. No doubt about it. A five point major would be up for grabs today.

She leaned back in her seat, painfully aware she was one of those little old ladies in big cars who could barely see over the steering wheel. Her mind should have been focused on what was ahead for today, but she couldn't stop thinking she should have given McCreery a chance at Westminster. Then nobody would be able to match Umpawaug's record, not even Hannah. Well, too late now.

"Too late for what?" Benny asked, jerking his head around in time to see a sad look flicker across her face.

She hadn't realized she had spoken out loud. "Nothing," she fibbed. "No, not nothing. Dreams left unfinished. That's what growing old is all about, son. Then one day, almost without warning, the ordinary things a person used to do without a single thought, like spreading toothpaste on a toothbrush or opening a jar — things that were cause for celebration as a young child — become hard again, and doing them a little longer is the only thing left because all the dreams are gone."

He began tapping his heels together. "Hey, I thought dog shows were supposed to be fun. I don't mean to be rude, but old people's brains must kind of dry up or something because all they do is talk about the good old days. Well, I'm here to tell you, being young isn't all it's cracked up to be."

She stared at him over the top of her glasses, and he thought for sure she was going to land them in a gully. Even when she was paying attention, he was afraid her big old clunker wouldn't make it around the steep, windy curves. His mother said Redding's roads were nothing but paved-over trails that cows had cut through the woods when they trotted back to their farms for milking in the olden days, and Benny thought it must be true. His classmates Chad and Eric were crazy about roller coasters and loved the way Redding's roads twisted and turned, plunging down sudden hills, but personally, his stomach could have used a rest right now. He'd had to gobble his breakfast so he wouldn't be late, and the cold sausage and pepperoni pizza wasn't sitting too well on his stomach.

"I don't recall mentioning anything about the good old days, or did my dried-up old brain forget? In case you're interested, age has nothing to do with it. Plenty of people scarcely older than you are old already."

He had no answer, and they drove in silence until they passed Stormfield, the home where Mark Twain had died. He had heard that Mark Twain was born under Halley's comet and died the next time it appeared seventy years later. He hoped it wasn't due again for a while. "What about dying? Do old people think about that a lot?"

"Not my favorite subject."

He slid back in his seat. "Mine, either."

She glanced out of the corner of her eye. "Don't worry. Your mother makes bad choices, but I don't think she's going to die any time soon."

He wiped his finger under his nose, hoping she wouldn't notice. Something tickled the back of his neck. He reached behind and felt Breaker's cool, wet nose.

"What's he doing?"

"Saying he likes you. I should've put him in his crate, but I got tired of chasing him around and used the seat belt instead."

Benny looked out the window. Only the hum of the car's engine interrupted the silence. A herd of black-and-white milk cows huddled together under an old apple tree. On the side of a red barn, hay was stacked in a mound. "Not to change the subject, but do you think we'll be on TV tonight if Breaker wins?"

"TV? Good grief, no. Quinnipiac's not that big. Maybe a story in *The New Haven Register.*

"I'm pretty sure he'll win. Everyone says Umpawaug poodles are the best in the world. Even Mona."

The car swerved again. "She does?"

"Sure, as long as you're not around." He turned and stared out the window. A weather-beaten vegetable stand, the work of some farmer, stood unattended. "Sweet corn, three dollars a dozen" was painted on a hand-lettered sign. He had one more question. "Bess, do you think I'm one of those young people who's old already?"

"Why do you ask?"

"Because I wish for things I can never have. Like for my dad and my mom to be married again. We'd all live together in one big house — Sonya, too — and I'd never have to miss anyone ever again." He hung his head. "I guess that's dumb?"

She didn't answer.

He tapped his foot. "Sorry, sorry, Bess. I didn't mean it about old people's brains."

She waved a forgiving hand. "I'm not mad. I don't know the answer." A slow smile crept across her lips. "Like I would. Me, who's spent my whole life wishing for something just out of reach."

They snuck a peek at each other and laughed. Breaker wriggled excitedly, too, wanting to be in on the act.

He grinned. "I guess we are kind of alike."

She flexed her fingers and steered with her palms, a bittersweet smile on her face. "A couple of wishful thinkers."

He settled back in his seat. The same sad look Bess had worn earlier came and wrapped itself around Benny, but he was looking out the window and nobody saw.

Chapter 36

Bess eased the car into the parking spot marked "Reserved for Officers" and led the way to the section of the field house where standard poodles traditionally set up their grooming tables. She took the last empty space up front. Hannah and her dogs were comfortably settled at the opposite end. Breaker and Chicory would go head to head against each other for the first time today. Either dog could win, but over their lifetime careers, the one with the greater heart would come out on top.

Bess spotted Nancy Valentine, an old friend, who waved and hurried over. As usual, Nancy was elegantly turned out, this time in a yellow halter dress with a designer label. Bess had avoided spilling half her coffee down the front of her polo shirt, but her glen plaid pants could have used a good press after sitting in the car.

Bess peeked in Nancy's handbag where her champion toy poodle had been known to travel. "Pipe Dream not here today?"

Nancy shook her head. Her Julie Andrews hairdo swirled back into place perfectly. "I'm judging toys, remember?"

Bess urged Benny forward and said, "This is Benny Neusner. He's doing the honors today."

Nancy gave the pubescent boy the once-over. A new pimple decorated the middle of his forehead. She raised her eyebrows at Bess, inviting an explanation that didn't come. She reached down and gave Breaker a pat on the head. "Hoping for a second major today?" she asked, straightening up. "This handsome puppy could do it. He's the image of McCreery at that age."

Breaker was so pleased by the compliment that he hopped up on Nancy's spotless dress before Benny could pull him off. He gasped and waited to see what she would do.

She squeezed Breaker's muzzle like he was good enough to eat and brushed off invisible paw prints. "Don't worry. With two toys and a standard at home, I'm used to a few smudges now and then."

Benny felt a tug on the lead and saw Felix and Chicory approaching. Except for Chicory's black coat, he wouldn't have known him from Breaker.

Felix bussed the ladies' cheeks and shook hands with Benny.

"I suppose Hannah's bringing half the kennel again today?" Bess asked, giving Breaker's handsome littermate the once-over.

Felix grinned slyly. He and Bess were friends, but they were rivals, too. "Besides Chicory? Just another puppy from Susie's litter, a girl named Crumpet. Hannah's in a hurry to finish her and begin breeding those beautiful Umpawaug faces. Not that she won't wait a couple of years for Crumpet to mature."

Benny rocked back on his heels. "Chicory must be worried about going up against Breaker. He won a major at Housatonic, remember?"

Felix smiled so broadly he forgot to disguise his overbite. "It wouldn't surprise me if both these dogs finished their championships in puppy trim like their father."

Benny wrinkled his nose. "I still don't know why everyone gets so excited about a dog being a champion. I think Breaker looks nice no matter what."

Bess and Felix exchanged an amused look. "Let's put it this way," Felix said. "Only finished champions get invited to Westminster."

Benny's eyes grew round with understanding. "Oh."

Bess gave a quick glance at the littermates who were busy inspecting each other's credentials in a series of undignified sniffs. "Aren't you getting a bit ahead of yourself? We've both seen gorgeous puppies turn into pet material when they hit adolescence."

"Well, these two both look like winners today," Nancy said. "All I can say is I'm glad I'm not judging."

Benny looked around. "Speaking of winning, where are the reporters?"

"Never mind the reporters. Keep your eye on Breaker," Bess snapped, embarrassed the boy's inexperience was hanging out like stained underwear on a clothesline.

Felix cleared his throat for an announcement and waited until everyone's eyes were on him. "Hannah has important news. She'll fill in the details, but I can't wait. They caught the guy that stole McCreery. He's confessed to everything."

Bess gasped and steadied herself on Benny's arm. Breaker looked from one to the other, a worried frown between his eyes.

Felix pulled Chicory in closer. "After what happened to McCreery, Hannah installed a silent alarm and motion detector floodlights. I happened to be there when the thief arrived, and we had him down on the ground before he had time to finish his story. His van had a dented right fender, by the way."

Benny banged his fist into his palm. "I wish I'd been there. I'd have taught him a lesson he'd never forget."

"The guy runs a puppy mill," Felix continued. "Apparently, he was trying to add a little quality to his stock.

The police have closed him down, thank goodness."

Bess signaled Benny it was time to move on. He kept a tight grip on the lead as Breaker pranced and bobbed his way through the section where merchants had set up booths filled with all kinds of dog toys and paraphernalia. He was thinking about buying a deck of cards with pictures of dogs to show the kids at school when a loud cheer coming from the agility ring caught his ear. He turned to see a border collie heading toward the apex of a sort of teepee like an Olympic swimmer mounting the high dive. Breaker caught the excitement and began pulling in that direction.

"Go, ahead," Bess said. "We can watch for a minute."

They moved closer to ringside for a better view of an Australian sheep dog, its body quivering in anticipation, poised at the start of the obstacle course. The handler, a boy a year or two older than Benny, wearing blue overalls, gave the signal to start. The dog charged up and down a ramp, dove off the top into a tunnel, dashed out the other end, and zigzagged through a series of poles. Each step of the way, the boy moved smoothly along at the dog's side, giving hand signals and whispering words of encouragement. They reached the finish line like a cleanup batter sliding for home plate. The dog jumped into the boy's arms, her tail wagging joyfully. The boy hugged her back with a gap-toothed grin.

"Awesome!" Benny exclaimed over the applause of the crowd.

A cut-down cream standard poodle was waiting to go next. Benny turned to Bess. "Did you ever enter an Umpawaug poodle in agility or obedience?"

She nodded at Breaker dancing on his hind legs in the direction of an attractive King Charles spaniel. "What do you think? Poodles are great athletes and natural-born show-offs so they do well in both, but I stuck with conformation." She hesitated. "Years ago, I considered entering one of my bitches in field trials along with the Labradors and other retrievers. She would dive into bone-chilling water after anything that flew quicker than any dog I ever knew, but I got busy with other priorities and never followed through."

He reeled Breaker back in, straining at the effort. "People like my dad think conformation classes are just overblown beauty pageants."

She scowled. "There's a little more to them. Conformation started decades ago as a way for experts to identify the dogs with the best traits, so their genes could be passed on to the next generation."

The show steward called for Breaker's class, and Benny found his place in line. The judge was Winston Samish, one of the grand old men in the poodle game. He and Bess had co-owned a dog a few years ago, but he wouldn't let friendship enter into his decision today.

Winston told Breaker and the six other dogs to circle the ring once and then line up along the side. Because Hannah had gotten her entry in early, Chicory and Felix were first to be called. Felix was a veteran handler with a puppy to match, making Breaker's brother the hands-on favorite. He went through his paces flawlessly, showing off his perfect manners. Winston gave him one last look and called the next dog forward.

Benny's heart pounded while he waited for the other four puppies to be examined, but at last it was Breaker's turn. He stood like a statue while Winston examined him from nose to tail. He even let Winston raise his lips to check his mouth without moving a muscle. Winston jotted down a couple of notes and then ordered Benny to take Breaker up to the far end of the ring, turn, and bring him back down again.

From his first step, Breaker seemed to do everything right. Tail straight, head high, he sashayed his funny little butt from one end of the ring to the other. He seemed to be telling the other hopefuls, "Better luck next time." Only the future would tell whether Breaker would carry McCreery's prize-winning features into adulthood, but looks aren't the whole story in the show ring. The thrill of center stage, a passion for pleasing the crowd, the lure of the spotlight can occasionally thrust even a mediocre dog into the winner's circle, and Breaker was far from mediocre.

Winston ordered Benny to take Breaker down to the end of the ring and back for a second look. "I'm in charge, I'm in charge," Benny whispered, trying to remember everything Bess had taught him. All those practice sessions were really paying off! Breaker was taking to his show career like he was born to it. He pranced along cheerfully at Benny's side, watching closely for any signal. When they made the final turn and came around to face Winston again, Benny was sure they were in the running.

But the contest wasn't finished. Winston walked down the line one more time. He studied Chicory, then Breaker, back and forth between the brown and black littermates. He signaled Chicory to step out of line and trot around the ring once more. Felix held the lead loosely and Chicory moved forward. The puppy's joy at being in the ring shone through in the jaunty lift of his head and the delicate way his feet barely touched the ground. He seemed to be reminding the world that he was an Umpawaug poodle, too.

They made the final turn and were heading down the last stretch, when out of nowhere, Felix seized up with a monstrous sneeze. Chicory broke his gait and looked up at Felix anxiously.

A disappointed groan traveled through the spectators. At the biggest shows, a tiny fraction separated the winners and losers. Still, Quinnipiac wasn't quite in that league. Felix pulled himself together and finished his tour around the ring, taking his place at the head of the line. It was all over except for Winston's decision.

Winston squared his shoulders and glanced at the judges' table. Resting on top along with the official trophies was the American Kennel Club record book where the winner's name would be preserved for all time. He turned to the show steward and reached for the small stack of ribbons. He held the blue one out ostentatiously in front and walked to the center of the ring.

"First!" he shouted in a loud voice and pointed straight at Chicory.

Bess couldn't hear Winston shout "Second!" over the applause, but she saw him point at Breaker and hand Benny a red ribbon. She pushed through the crowd, past the show photographer posing the winner. A beaming Hannah stood in the middle with Felix and Chicory on one side of her and Winston on the other.

Benny was in the grooming area, blinking back tears, his arms wrapped around Breaker's neck. "Sorry, Bess, sorry. I've let you and Breaker down."

The dog did look miserable. A good show dog wants to win with every fiber of his being, and it seemed Breaker was as disappointed as Benny.

"Nonsense," she insisted brusquely, ruffling Breaker's topknot. "No telling what makes a judge pick one dog over another. One favors heads, another the set of the tail. Some won't put a brown up over a black." She reached and pulled the red ribbon out of Benny's blazer pocket where he had stuck it. She ran it through her fingers tenderly, as if she didn't have a closet full of others, not to mention solid silver trophies. She studied it, debating, and thrust it at Benny. "Here, you keep it."

He wiped his nose on his sleeve. He studied her face and was reassured by the encouragement he saw there. "I guess it's not so bad."

"Chicory was lucky today. Another day will be Breaker's

turn. There's plenty of time for him to earn all the points he needs."

He gave her a weak smile.

"That's better. What do you say we give him another chance at Bar Harbor over Labor Day? I'll be back from my trip with Mona before then, and a second major will be up for grabs. You can be sure Chicory will be there."

Breaker placed his paws on Benny's chest and grinned into his face.

He ruffled his topknot. "You'd like that, wouldn't you, boy?" He turned to Bess with a grin. "You're right. Plenty of time. We'll show Chicory how it's done in Bar Harbor. Just see if we don't."

Chapter 37

Kate heard a knock on her office door and checked her watch. It must be David. He had phoned this morning with an idea he wanted to discuss. She had tried putting him off. She had too much on her mind to spar with him, but when he said it was about the school, she yielded.

She waved him to a chair and sat in her usual spot. "You had an idea?" she prompted, getting right down to business. His amused smile told her he expected no less.

He followed her lead and came straight to the point. "Benny's told me all about the teachers' theme for summer school. 'A Day at the Circus' sounds like fun, and I was thinking a striped tent and a cotton candy machine would take it up a notch. Maybe add a pony ride."

She cocked her head. "No doubt, but those things aren't exactly in our budget."

He waved away her objection. "I'd like to donate them. You probably have a whole list of things the school needs, but I want to do this for the kids. It could be kind of a 'thank you' to the teachers, too, adding a little zip to their hard work."

"Well, yes …"

A "but" was coming and he interrupted. "Please, I'll write another check for an equal amount, and you can spend it any way you want."

She leaned back and laughed. "I usually don't have people begging to give the school money."

"My pleasure. If it makes you smile like this, I might have to do it more often."

They fell into an awkward silence, both of them wondering whether he was really doing it for the school, or for Benny, or maybe even for her?

"Benny's asked if he can bring the dogs and do a circus act with them. Bess is fine with it, but I told him he needed to check with you." He grinned. "See, I'm learning. He needs to speak for himself."

She smiled, but the worry when he mentioned Benny must have shown on her face.

He leaned forward. "Problem?"

She dropped her chin. She knew the boy was hiding something, but he wouldn't say what. She only hoped he hadn't gotten into something over his head. "You know I can't discuss him," she said, but there was no sting in it.

"Benny's a good kid. Whatever it is, I think we can trust him."

Her eyes moved over his face, as if trying to read the man he truly was.

He reached for her hand, and she didn't pull away. He fingered her filigree bracelet tenderly, perhaps remembering she had worn it the day they met. "I'll keep an eye on him. I know you can't tell me anything, but I'll let you know if I learn something."

His hand around hers felt warm and gentle and strong enough to keep her safe. She longed to lace her fingers through his and hold on forever. "Thank you," she said, freeing her hand.

He exhaled deeply, a shift in the wind. "So, now that that's settled, what about dinner? I make a mean beef stroganoff or we can go out."

She rose and crossed her arms protectively across

her heart. All her instincts warned her against becoming involved with him. Yes, he was attractive. Yes, he was intelligent. Yes, he seemed kind, but there was always the possibility of heartbreak ahead. He was inviting her to step into a loosely moored boat wearing the wrong shoes. Would he grab her hand and pull her to safety, or would she fall into the roiling waters and sink?

"I'm not very good at dinners," she said.

He turned on his heel, the tips of his ears reddening. "I'll call your secretary for an appointment."

She shivered, like a ghost was walking over her grave. In a way, he was a ghost, a phantom reminder of feelings long dormant inside her. She had vowed never to leave herself open to that kind of hurt again, and now, after years of building a protective wall around her well-ordered life, he threatened to tear it down. How could she be sure the ending would be different with him? She couldn't. No one could tell the future. Isn't that what she told her clients? David had been patient, but now he was walking away, maybe for good. Perhaps what Benny had told her was true. She needed more in her life. Benny trusted the man. Why shouldn't she?

"Wait," she called at David's back. "A man who crunches numbers and cooks? How can I turn that down?"

He spun around. His face relaxed into a smile. In his mind's eye, he pictured her sitting across from him at a candlelit table overlooking the waterfall at Cob's Mill Inn. "Spinning Wheel? Seven o'clock?"

She returned a real smile. "Seven."

CHAPTER 38

Breaker dragged Benny along behind him, obedience lessons flown out the window. Bess was back from her trip and somehow the puppy sensed they were on their way to see her.

Benny rapped on the kitchen door and entered without waiting for an answer. He looked around the kitchen, and his chin dropped disappointedly. Bess was seated alone, a month's worth of unopened mail in front of her. "Where's McCreery?" he asked.

Breaker couldn't care less where his illustrious father was hiding. He lunged across the room and landed halfway on Bess's lap.

Bess put her arms around his neck and talked around his poodle kisses. "McCreery's fine, just asleep upstairs, probably in Mona's bed. They became great pals on the trip."

She gave Breaker a final pat and urged him back down on the floor. She picked up a dog magazine and began flipping through the pages. The lead story about Fandango, Picture Perfect Pete's star offspring, threatened her mood. "If Fandango has the snappy temperament of his father, it won't help the gene pool for him to be receiving all this attention."

Benny shrugged. "Breaker will take care of that. He'll

beat Fandango at Bar Harbor, and then people will figure out which dog deserves to be on the cover of *Dog World.*"

"Knock, knock," David called, opening the kitchen door. He nodded at Benny and stood back to give his mother the once-over. "The trip's done you good. Your color's back." He buzzed the top of her head and gently brushed the sleeve of her shirt. "You and Mona must have done some shopping. Pretty, I always liked aqua on you."

Bess poured a glass of milk and handed it to Benny, while David poured two cups of coffee. He reached for a small pitcher shaped like a one-eyed pirate's head and added cream from the rim of a tri-cornered hat. "How was Mona's condo?"

Bess shrugged. "It was all right."

Benny and David exchanged knowing smiles. They both were convinced Mona would never move without Bess, and Bess would never leave Redding.

David sipped his coffee. "We've been rehearsing with Breaker almost every afternoon, haven't we, Benny? And practicing the times tables, too."

Hearing his name, Breaker pranced over to her. Now that he wasn't jumping all over her, she could take a closer look at him. Her hands moved across his back and down his legs. She turned pale and leaned heavily against the table.

David rushed to her side and placed his hands on her shoulders to support her. "Bess? Mother?"

Benny followed Bess's gaze and wondered how he had missed the change. In the month she had been gone, Breaker had morphed into an all-together different dog. His legs were too long, his neck was too short, and his back sloped down like a whippet's. His feet, while still quick, no longer landed in steps so light a prima ballerina would perform as a dancing eggplant to have them. Only his face kept the distinctive Umpawaug features of his ancestors.

Blood pounded in Benny's ears. "It's just that awkward

adolescent stage? Breaker can still go to Westminster, right?" He looked down at his own overgrown feet and winced.

She picked up the *Dog World* and tossed it into the trash. "Don't let your imagination run away with you."

David reached for the leash. "I'll keep Breaker at home with me a little while longer."

Bess turned her back, her dream of Westminster fading like disappearing ink. "Do whatever you want. You will anyway. Sell him as a pet. That would be the kindest."

Outside, Benny hunkered down and took the puppy's head between his hands. "It'll be all right, you'll see," he said, putting on a smile he didn't feel. Then he remembered Bess's expression and dropped the cheerful act like an overfilled sack. Unless a miracle happened, Breaker would never stand in the winner's circle again.

Chapter 39

No matter how sad Benny felt about Breaker, he was sure Bess felt worse. As her partner, the least he could do was drop by and try to cheer her up. He found her in the puppy shed with McCreery on top of the grooming table. He held the *New Hope School Gazette* up and read the headline in a voice loud enough to be heard over the buzz of the clippers: "Champion Poodle is New Hope School's Neighbor."

She snapped off the clippers and rubbed a stray clump of poodle hair off her nose with her sleeve. She reached for the paper. "Hmmm, an interesting drawing of McCreery by Christopher, age six. Such pretty blue eyes. And a feature article on the famous Umpawaug Kennels by Carol Gale." She squinted at the class picture. "Which one is she?"

He ignored her question and pointed to the photo of him with his arm around McCreery. "My teacher took it with her digital camera and put it on our school website where everyone in the world can see it. My mother will be as excited as me."

"Nice," she said, dropping it on the counter. She turned her back and reached for McCreery's brush. The swishing sound it made moving across the dog's coat was the only noise in the room.

He hopped up on the counter where Breaker had come

back to life eight months ago and raised his feet over his head, back against the wall. He pulled the red ribbon he and Breaker had won at Quinnipiac out of his pocket and rested it against his chest, tracing the floret with his finger. "Feels like my mother's favorite blouse," he said to himself. He stuck it back in his pocket and straightened up. "I'm bored."

She handed him the brush. "Here, McCreery would love you to finish grooming him. Believe me, I've got plenty to keep me busy." She sat on the rusty folding chair and picked up the newspaper again.

He tossed the brush back into the tattered shoe box with the other grooming aids. "McCreery only likes me because I'm young. He can't help it if you're all worn out."

She flushed. Last week at Betty Johnson's Beauty Boutique, a lady who had to be every day of sixty years old raced to open the door for her like she was a helpless old lady who couldn't kick it open with her shoe anymore.

He rolled the ends of the red ribbon into tight circles and let them drop. "My body may be stronger than yours, but how'd you like to have so many feelings they make your head swim?"

She smiled sadly. "We have something in common. Neither of our bodies does everything we want."

"At least your brain's working."

She shuddered. Lately, she'd been afraid whenever she forgot something. Had she always been like that, only now she noticed it more? Mona would know.

He came around to the front of the grooming table and grabbed hold of McCreery's chin. He turned the old champion's head this way and that, his brows drawn together in deep concentration. Satisfied, he let go of the dog and turned to Bess.

"Wait a minute! I have an idea," he almost shouted in his excitement. "How old's McCreery?"

Hearing his name, the dog's ears twitched. He seemed to sense something important was in the works.

"McCreery? He must be about ten."

His face fell. "Years? That's pretty old for a dog, isn't it?"

She stood and fished the brush out of the box. "Not that old — at least for an Umpawaug poodle."

He spun around on one leg and came back all smiles like a puppet head with a different face painted on each side. "Breaker may be ruined, but McCreery's still a great-looking dog. You said so yourself."

"So what?" she asked, sounding juvenile. She knew where he was heading.

McCreery seemed to know, too. He jumped off the grooming table, shook out his coat, and positioned himself the way he had done dozens of times in front of a judge.

"So we could take McCreery to Westminster."

She froze in place. Only her eyes moved, stopping on the red second place ribbon. "Westminster? You think I'm still thinking about Westminster?"

He flicked out his hands, his neck thrust out like a turtle's. "Du-uh! Remember what you told me on the way to Quinnipiac? Westminster's been your dream your whole life. So why didn't you ever try?"

She jerked her head back like she had been hit. "Plenty of reasons, that's why."

"Maybe you should figure it out."

She pulled her thick eyebrows together. She ordered McCreery into an empty crate and banged the door shut. "Dream time's over."

He stared at his feet and swallowed hard. A bitter taste in his mouth made him want to punch somebody. Instead, he slipped his fingers through the grate of McCreery's crate and gave him a little scratch. "Sorry, boy, I tried."

Chapter 40

The autumn day was crisp and warm, and a blanket of colorful leaves covered New Hope School's playground faster than the Nature Club could rake them. Recently, Kate had assigned Benny to help out as a kind of lunchtime aid in the primary class, and she decided she ought to see how it was going. So far, Benny enjoyed being the "big kid," and the children loved his attention, but what she heard when she opened the door burst her bubble.

"Look, Dr. Kate! Margaret's eating boogers again," Benny announced in a self-satisfied voice. Heads popped up all over the classroom, waiting to see what would happen next.

Joel wrapped his hands around his neck and stuck out his tongue. "Gross!"

"Gross," repeated George, depositing his own nose booty down the side of his jeans.

Kate sighed and glanced at Margaret scrunched down in her chair. The girl's thick hair fell over her face, a shield against a prying world. Both arms were pocked by open sores where she had worried the skin away.

"What are you boys supposed to be doing?" Kate asked, encompassing Joel and George in one glance. "And Benny, you're supposed to be a leader, not tattling on people." She passed by Margaret's desk and dropped a clean tissue.

"Here," she whispered, "and try not to pick at those scabs."

On Mrs. Santos's signal, the children rushed into the kitchen and jockeyed for their favorite seats. Out of the corner of her eye, Kate noticed Keisha passing half her cupcake to Margaret. Kate smiled. The children could be a handful, but there was a reason why they were called "special."

A loud thud jolted her out of her reverie. Benny was on his feet, his chair tipped over behind him. He was holding a Styrofoam container over his head ready to dump. To his left, Keisha was frozen in fear. To his right, Sammy took shelter under the table.

Kate moved in front of him, protecting the other children. "What's going on?" she asked, keeping one eye on the container.

"Sonya and my dad had a date at the Thai restaurant in Westport last night, and she gave me their leftovers for lunch."

"You can have half my sandwich," Jacob piped up bravely. "It's good — peanut butter and jelly."

Benny started to lower the box. None of the other children moved.

Kate stood quietly in place. "How about we invite your dad and Sonya to one of our meetings?"

He studied his shoes. His lower lip quivered, and she thought the crisis had passed.

Before he could speak, the door burst open, and Clarence from Mr. Chang's room dashed in, his long stringy hair swinging back and forth. He crouched down, trying to hide the wet splotch on the front of his pants. "Forgot my book," he explained lamely and crab-crawled to the bathroom.

Kate held out her phone, but the mood was broken. Before she could stop him, Benny dashed out the door. He had only gone a few yards when he skidded to a stop. A poodle was lying on the grass in front of him with his legs splayed in the air like a Thanksgiving turkey.

"McCreery!" he shouted and held out his arms. The poodle leaped to his feet and careened toward him, ears flapping, mouth open in a wide grin. Before Benny could duck, the dog made a direct hit against his chest. Benny windmilled his arms and managed to keep his balance.

The class had been drawn by the noise and gathered at the door. Only Sammy stood back and clung to Kate. His feet danced up and down in place and his hands slapped his sides.

"Sammy's a sissy, Sammy's a sissy," George teased.

While the other students guffawed and pointed, the poodle ran in figure eights from Benny to the others and back again. Each time the dog circled back, Benny grabbed for his collar, but the dog was too quick.

"Hey, Dr. Kate," Benny called. "McCreery's acting weird."

Taking advantage of the distraction, the poodle charged and collided against Benny's chest with a thud. Benny staggered back and almost landed on the ground. The dog leaned in to lick Benny's face, and Benny got his chance. "Gotcha," he said, snagging the dog's collar, and looked at his classmates for applause. The dog made a sidewise leap and twisted free. Benny stared at his empty hand. "I had him," he whimpered.

"I'll catch him," Margaret called from the classroom door. She had been hanging out in the bathroom when the commotion started. She zipped up her culottes and headed for the excited dog. She crouched and held out her hand. "Good doggie, it's all right," she crooned.

The poodle flopped over on his back like he had hit a glass wall. Four walnut-shaped feet stuck up in the air like a giant dead insect's. Margaret slipped beside him and rubbed his belly. If a dog could purr, he would have.

Benny heard a noise behind him and turned. A second brown poodle was heading toward the classroom. Bess was right behind him. She was holding a rectangular pan covered with aluminum foil. "Mona made devil's food cake for Funhouse Friday," she called, unaware of the commotion.

Benny looked back and forth between the two dogs, a puzzled expression on his face. "If that's McCreery," he said, pointing with his chin at the dog beside her, "who's this?" He tipped his hand at the dog now sitting politely at his side.

Bess stepped closer and signaled the dog to stand. Her eyes grew wide. She walked around the dog slowly, studying him as if she had never seen him before. She handed Benny the cake pan and wrapped her arms around the dog's neck.

Benny's mouth dropped open. For a minute he couldn't speak. Then he turned to the other students like a master of ceremonies. "Hey, guys, Breaker's got his looks back! We're going to Westminster!"

Kate stepped forward and gave a warning cough.

Benny turned to Bess. "Right, Bess? I'm going to be on TV?"

She straightened up, avoiding his eyes. "We'll see."

He jammed his fist in the air. "Yes!"

Kate watched Bess head toward home with both dogs following close behind. She was happy for Benny, and Bess, too. She even imagined there was a new spring in the old woman's step. Still, she couldn't help wondering. Had she really heard a little catch in Bess's voice when Benny mentioned Westminster?

Chapter 41

David knocked on his mother's back door with his knee and prepared to wait. It was early and she might still be asleep, but she opened the door promptly, fully dressed in corduroy slacks and a blouse with a sweater vest. He brushed past her with something hidden under a green checkered dish towel.

She lifted the towel and peeked. The aroma of warm blueberry muffins wafted up to her. She cast a suspicious look at him. "Beware the Greeks and all that."

"Careful, they're still hot. I know how much you like them."

She arched an eyebrow. "Overnight guest?"

"I wish! No, I made them myself. Even picked the blueberries and saved them in the freezer for a special occasion." He stuck his head in the fridge and called out, "Any real butter in here? I'm not thinking about cholesterol while I can smell those muffins."

"Probably hidden behind the heavy cream," she said, prying two muffins out.

He thought she was kidding, but there it was. He pulled out a chair and sat. "I heard about Breaker. Fantastic!" He crossed his legs and looked at her. "What's next?" She studied him over the top of her glasses. "I'm surprised you're so interested. I thought you'd drop the act once you got me to keep Breaker."

He flinched. "It's not an act."

She set two plates on the table, poured the coffee, and sat, too. She was stalling for time. She met his eyes, struggling shyly to hold his gaze. "You mean it, don't you?"

He reached across the table and covered her hand with his own. "I love you. When are you going to get it?"

She let it rest there a moment and then withdrew gently. "Sometimes I wonder if it would have been better if I'd taken you with me all those times on the road."

He stood and retrieved the coffee pot and topped off their cups. "Benny's got you thinking, too, hasn't he? Watching him makes me remember the times you were gone. Not that Mona wasn't wonderful, but still …"

"… I'm your mother," she finished for him.

"Yes," he said, "but now I see your point of view. Like you said, I was never interested in dogs except for what they meant to you. I hated junior showmanship. And spending night after night in hotel rooms, always missing school, never having friends? That's no life for a kid."

"That's what I thought," she whispered, her gravelly voice shaky, "but now when I see how lonely Benny is, hanging around every afternoon like — well, like a dog — hoping his mother will pay him some attention."

He sat again and faced her, his shoulders squared confidently. "The difference is I knew where you were. You'd be home when you said." He hesitated. "Not that I wasn't afraid you loved your dogs more than me."

She winced. She had worried about that for years.

He drew in a bracing breath and leaned forward. "I might as well go ahead and say it. Lately, I've had the idea that you never went to Westminster because you felt guilty about the way you treated me."

She waved her hand dismissively. "You've been spending too much time with Benny's shrink."

He crossed his arms protectively, but now that he'd said it, he wouldn't take it back. "No, really. I've watched your face when you look at Benny. Every time his mother lets him down, it almost breaks your heart. I think it's about you and me."

She closed her eyes, shutting him out. Her head rocked back and forth in silent denial. All those times she had tried and failed to give Westminster a try were just coincidences. She tried to speak, to tell him so, but her mouth was dry and no words came.

"Forgive yourself. I have," he said. He turned and walked to the window, swallowing the feelings that would have crushed them both.

She pressed the heel of her palm against her forehead, hoping to still the jumbled thoughts tumbling around her brain. Could he be right? Had she been holding back all those years because of a bizarre notion she was repaying him for all the times she had neglected him and put her dogs first? She had heard people could stab themselves in the back and not even know it, but she never imagined it could happen to her.

She reached behind her for the silver cup that had rested on the kitchen counter ever since Benny returned it. She tilted it back and forth, like she was trying to read a faint message etched inside, and then placed it in front of the chair where the boy always sat. He would find it there the next time he came.

David pulled back the kitchen curtain. "I'm surprised the dogs aren't in here sniffing around for a muffin."

She brushed at her cheeks with both hands and straightened up in her chair.

"Mona's taken them both to Putnam Park. Some charity event or other."

They shared a smile. It was so like Mona to fuss at Bess about raising dogs and then co-opt them for a pet project.

He started to leave, nodding at the muffins on the counter. “I’ll pick up the muffin tin next time I come.”

“Sure you won’t take a couple? Maybe share them with someone?”

“If you mean Kate, I wouldn’t mind.” He studied his toes, looking boyish. “I like the whole package: the woman, the school, the kids. I think I might have found my own special passion. I admit Mona’s not the only one who’s envied you that.”

She rose and gave him a quick hug, something she hadn’t done for years. “Go on, get out of here. I can’t sit around here all day chatting about muffins. I’ve got dogs to take care of.”

Chapter 42

Bess shook herself awake and checked the clock on the mantle. Four fifteen. She must have fallen asleep on the sofa after two blueberry muffins at lunch. Last year's PCA catalogue lay open on her chest. She had been reading her ad. For thirty years she had altered the lyrics of an old show tune to announce Umpawaug's news. What would this year bring? "Happy Days are Here Again" or "Fools Rush In"? Breaker wasn't the first Umpawaug puppy that had transformed a mismatch of adolescent bones into a stunning maturity, but no one knew yet whether his old sparkle and determination to win had returned along with his looks. The Liberty Bell would tell the tale. If he did well, he might just finish his championship in time.

She heard the rattle of Mona's key in the lock and shuffled to the kitchen in her stocking feet. McCreery and Breaker slipped through and hurried to sniff their dinner bowls. It was too early for their supper, but it never hurt to try.

The surprise was Mona. She was wearing a long brown skirt covered by a coarse blue apron. A red petticoat stuck out underneath. A homespun blouse, brown shawl, and white colonial cap with a black ribbon tied in front topped off her outfit.

Bess staggered back and pressed a hand against her

chest. "What in the world?"

Mona smiled cheerily and stepped inside. "It's the annual Patriots' Weekend at Putnam Park. We're doing a living museum all about life in General Putnam's camp and how he helped George Washington defeat the British. Lots of cannons and stuff. Very historical." She shifted a black iron kettle from one wrist to the other and waited for her sister's response.

Bess looked her twin up and down. She recognized the scent of the perfume Mona had given her for their birthday. "And you're supposed to be a camp follower?"

Mona flounced her red petticoat and reached for a muffin on the counter. "Very funny, but thanks for letting me take the dogs. A few boys preferred climbing on the cannons, but the others wished they could take Breaker and McCreery home. One little girl even followed us to the car. She reminded me of you as a kid."

"Those dogs like nothing better than showing off for a crowd," Bess grumbled.

Mona knew her twin was secretly pleased. "I suppose that's what makes them great competitors in the ring," she said with her mouth full.

Breaker raised up from the mat and rubbed his muzzle against Mona's skirt, hunting for crumbs. McCreery scooted out from under the table and nosed Breaker out of the way. Breaker resisted, but only for a second before stepping back, head and tail lowered.

"McCreery still insists on being top dog," Mona observed.

Bess flicked her eyebrows, surprised her sister noticed. "Normally, I wouldn't let two intact males live in the same house, but McCreery's managed to contain his jealousy and keep the peace, at least so far."

Mona polished off the last of her muffin. "I have to admit it's hard to tell father and son apart now that Breaker's got his looks back."

Bess yawned, feigning indifference. "McCreery has always gotten himself up for every big show."

"Big show? For McCreery? You can't be serious."

Bess shrugged nonchalantly. "Just the Parade of Champions where the old fellows strut their paces. A kind of Veterans Day parade for dogs. People want to see the top-producing stud dog of all time. Sixty-five champions — so far."

Mona bent over and pulled off a shoe. A pebble that had caught inside fell out and rolled under Bess's chair. "I bumped into David at the Putnam Park. He said you two had a good talk."

Bess stabbed the pebble with her toe. It spun across the room. McCreery considered chasing it and dropped his chin onto his front paws again. "We had a few words about Westminster. Things like that," she answered evasively.

Mona studied her twin closely. "Do you think you'll actually make it this time? You won't just be letting yourself down. It'll be Benny, too.

Bess nodded. "I know." She stared into space, cocooning into herself. "David says I never went to Westminster because I feel guilty about the way I treated him as a kid. I think he's been hanging around with Dr. Kate too much." She thrust out her chin, challenging a fight to conceal how much she wanted her twin's opinion — and how much she feared her son could be right.

A slow grin grew at the corners of Mona's mouth. "It could be something in our childhood. Personally, I've never had the slightest urge to take a poodle to Westminster."

Bess stood and threw up her hands. "Oh, for heaven's sake. You didn't think I was serious, did you? Freud!"

Mona walked to the counter and busied herself stacking dishes in the dishwasher to hide a smile. For whatever reason, Bess had changed. She didn't know why, except Benny was part of it and David, too. This year there wouldn't be any false starts. Her sister would make it to Westminster and handle the outcome, whatever happened. She was sure.

She closed the dishwasher with a bang and headed for the door. "I'm late. A few of us are in a tableau at Emma Goldhorn's Rest Home. Something to cheer up the old folks." She stopped and turned when she heard the staccato of dog kibbles hitting metal bowls. She watched Bess mix in three tablespoons of her secret champion-building formula while McCreery and Breaker stared up at her like she was a goddess. A slow smile appeared at the corners of Bess's mouth as her dogs bent over their dishes. She didn't even know she was doing it.

"My real estate agent called about my condo this morning," Mona said. "Something about the plumbing this time, I think."

A white cloth fell out of her pocket, and Bess bent down stiffly to retrieve it. She spread the handkerchief across her palm, studying the "M" their mother had painstakingly embroidered in pink. "Pretty," she said, handing it back. "Mine was blue. I lost it years back."

"It was a long time ago."

Their eyes met, remembering. The tenderness of the moment was too awkward for them both and passed quickly.

Bess opened the door and signaled her sister to go through first. McCreery roused himself and scooted past, nosing Breaker out of the way. The night air had an autumn chill, and the sky was black, no moon, only specks of blinking stars. She stood a long time in the driveway, watching the taillights on Mona's red sports car grow smaller and smaller, until they finally disappeared from view. She pulled her sweater tight across her chest and signaled the waiting dogs to follow her inside.

Chapter 43

Benny and Bess rested under a sugar maple in lawn chairs she had stowed in the back of the station wagon and looked out over the field where the Liberty Bell All-Breed Show was about to begin. Breaker stretched out on the metal grooming table, cooling his belly, and McCreery sat sedately on top of his crate. The shade of the ancient tree barely made a dent in the heat of Indian summer. It was the hottest October day on record, and when it was hot in Philadelphia, it wasn't just hot; it was sticky hot.

Benny stuffed the last of his Philly cheesesteak hoagie into his mouth and tossed the grease-soaked wrapper into a nearby can. Breaker twitched his nose as the paper sailed by, but decided it was too hot to bother and lay his head down again. McCreery didn't even sniff.

"It's a good thing my mother decided not to come. She's not used to all this heat," Benny said. He patted his stomach. "I sure could use a nice, cool Frosty Freeze to top off my sandwich."

Bess took a can of diet lemonade out of the ice chest and handed him one. "Nobody can control the weather, but it'll be murder on the dogs."

"Probably global warming," he suggested importantly. "My teacher will probably make me write an article about it for the *NHS Gazette.*"

"I suppose you'll have a lot of work to make up for missing school yesterday."

He shook his head. "Naw. They had a field trip to the Mark Twain Library. I've been there a million times. The yellowish papers with Mark Twain's real handwriting are sort of cool, but the rest of it is just a bunch of books."

She rose. She had something special to do, and she didn't need Benny nosing in on it. "I'm going to have a look around. Keep Breaker in the shade and work on his coat. His tail needs fluffing out."

He shook his hands and blew. "I think I'm getting blisters. I better take a break and come with you."

She was pretty sure he wanted to sneak down to the parking lot and see if a TV truck had shown up. She reached into the ice chest and dropped a few ice cubes into the dogs' water dish. "You stay here with Breaker. This is what they call a benched show. Dogs are supposed to be on exhibit when they're not in the ring, so the public can educate themselves about the different breeds."

"What about McCreery? The public can educate themselves on him."

She flashed a fake smile. "Good idea. The Parade of Champions isn't until the very end. I'll take him with me." She snapped her fingers and McCreery jumped off his crate. He rubbed his muzzle along Bess's side while she clipped on his lead.

Plenty of well-wishers stopped Bess along the way. A few recognized McCreery from the old days. He feigned the cool detachment of royalty until he spotted Felix bringing Chicory back from a potty break. McCreery ignored his handsome black son and pounced on Felix's chest with delighted abandon.

"McCreery!" Felix greeted, rubbing the dog's rump vigorously. McCreery wriggled happily. Felix turned to Bess. "If this old boy weren't in pet clip, I would have taken him for Breaker. He looks good enough for the show ring himself." Felix slid his glasses to the end of his nose. "You didn't, did you?"

She shook her head. "Parade of Champions."

"Well, I wouldn't put it past you. No telling what you'll do now that the gleam is back in your eye." He lifted his own lead over McCreery's head and handed Chicory off to her.

She circled the lovely black dog. No question about it. Breaker's littermate would be stiff competition. His black coat had grown in thick and dark, and the Umpawaug face held true. Breaker and Chicory hadn't squared off in the ring since Quinnipiac when Chicory had come out on top. She handed the lead back to Felix. "Nice. I'd be ashamed if McCreery didn't produce good-looking get."

McCreery snuck a peek out of the corner of his eye and assumed an air of indifference equal to Bess's.

"Hannah's got her heart set on a win today," Felix teased.

She didn't mind. Their long friendship didn't cancel the honest rivalry between them. It was different with Hannah. Impossible to believe someone could be that nice.

"The fire marshal sprayed the tent roof, but it's turning to steam," a new voice interjected. Jim Wren had slipped up behind them. DandyGirl sat sedately at his feet. Jim unscrewed the lid of a thermos, extracted an ice chip and held it out. DandyGirl took it delicately between her lips and slid it down her throat. "It feels like a hundred degrees under the tent. If too many people drop out, the five-point major will be broken."

"Hannah's heart will break," Felix said. "She's got her letter extoling Chicory's record stamped and ready to mail to Westminster."

"We'll see," Bess said with greater confidence than she felt. Felix had hit a nerve. Breaker and Chicory each had one major and needed a second. Breaker had lost a lot of time during his homely adolescent phase, and even if he won a major today, he would still need five more points to finish his championship. A major win for Chicory would bring his point count up to the required fifteen, including the two majors. Even so, a championship in itself was no guarantee of a spot at Westminster. A dog couldn't just turn up at Madison Square Garden; he had to be invited.

The top five dogs of every breed are invited automatically and given a deadline to respond. The remaining spots go to other Champions of Record on a first come, first served basis. Entries become open at an announced time, and there is always a bit of a scramble to get applications in quickly because places fill up fast. No one can be assured of a spot until an acceptance letter is in hand, and neither Chicory nor Breaker had even finished his championship.

McCreery tugged on the lead, and Bess turned to see Benny and Breaker skid to a halt, both panting heavily. She narrowed her eyes disapprovingly. Between the heat and Felix's goading, she was in no mood for their shenanigans. "I thought I told you to keep that dog cool and calm. He'll need to be brushed out all over again."

Breaker dropped to his belly and covered his face with his paws.

"Sorry," Benny apologized, not looking sorry at all. "I thought you'd want to know there's a car with *Philadelphia Inquirer* on the door but no TV van."

Jim stifled a smile and hurried off with DandyGirl. Felix and Chicory went next.

Benny frowned. "Where's Chicory going?"

"He's entered in The American-Bred class. Hannah and Felix must think that's his best chance. If Breaker and Chicory both win their classes, they'll get their rematch in Winners."

Benny puffed out his chest. "Breaker's got Chicory on the run."

She nodded at a handsome white poodle at the head of the line. His picture was on the latest issue of *Dog World*. "Maybe, or maybe Hannah's worried about that dog over there. Fandango is Picture Perfect Pete's son. You may have heard of him."

Bess stayed with Benny until he found his place in line and then hurried toward the judges' table. She made a habit of checking the judge's identity in advance, but this was the first time she had entered on purpose because of one. Reginald Hannaford had worked for her father back when they were both kids. He had moved to Birmingham, England, decades ago but stayed in the dog game. Now, after all those years, he was standing a few yards away. He was talking to a teenage girl holding a black standard poodle puppy in her arms. He said something, and the girl nodded back excitedly. It was like watching herself fifty-odd years ago. Today he would be judging her dog and wouldn't even know it.

She ducked behind a tree, hoping she wouldn't be noticed. There would be time to catch up later. She wasn't trying to influence Reginald's decision, not really. It was enough to know that a judge who shared her tastes would be picking the winner. After all, Reginald was the one who encouraged her to concentrate on breeding beautiful faces — as long as they went along with loving temperaments. Wasn't she counting on that today?

The show steward hastened over to Reginald and tapped his watch. Bubba Silverstein was famous for keeping his shows running like a Swiss train. With the weather preying on the dogs, he was the right man for the job.

She made her way to the grandstand and climbed over a sea of legs to find Jim's wife, Holly. An expectant silence filled the tent as Reginald stepped into the ring. His shirt was soaked to the skin as if he had been standing in a rainstorm.

"You'd think he would dispense with a tie in all this heat," Holly said, fanning herself with her catalogue.

"Not Reginald. A judge doesn't appear without a tie."

Holly looked at her curiously. "I didn't know you two were acquainted."

Bess made an elaborate display of sniffing the air. "This stadium smells like mildewed sailcloth without a nice ocean breeze to carry it off."

"The firemen sprinkled the roof earlier, but it's not helping. The temperature might have dropped a few degrees, but now the humidity's worse."

Breaker was first in line, followed by an unknown black dog, and then Fandango. Reginald's eyes widened when Benny appeared, apparently surprised by the boy's age, but he turned his attention to Breaker without comment. Breaker stood politely to be examined and went through his paces as instructed. He never put a foot down wrong; Benny just ran to keep up. In what seemed like only a minute, their turn was over.

Holly leaned into Bess's ear. "Benny's come a long way. You've taught him well, Bess."

Next came the black dog with an unfamiliar handler. Holly flipped through her catalogue for the pedigree. It was Breaker's other brother. Hannah must have sold him. Holly leaned over and whispered, "McCreery can't put out champions every time."

"He looks like a decent pet puppy to me."

The judge waved the dog off and called out Fandango.

Holly sighed. "Look at that gorgeous white coat."

What happened next was so quick Bess wasn't sure how it started. A dog was loose in the ring. Benny had the presence of mind to grasp Breaker's lead and hold on. Fandango's handler wasn't as quick. Fandango bolted free and grabbed the loose dog by the neck. Reginald and Fandango's handler dashed across the ring to break up the fight before either dog became seriously injured, but Fandango wouldn't let up even when his handler recovered the lead. He twisted and jerked, fighting to free himself. The handler yanked down hard on the lead. Fandango bared his teeth and lunged. The handler barely got his hand out of the way in time.

A horrified gasp rippled through the crowd. Bubba Silverstein stepped forward and excused Fandango from the ring.

"One more incident like that, and Fandango will be banned for good," Holly whispered.

Reginald decided he had seen enough. He pointed at Breaker and called, "First," in a loud voice. Breaker realized his work was done. Before Benny could stop him, the puppy planted a wet smacker on Reginald's lips.

Bess couldn't hold back a laugh. Reginald glanced her way. An almost imperceptible flick of the eye let her know he had recognized her. Her smile hadn't changed in fifty-odd years.

Reginald moved the other classes along in good time. Before long all the winners, including Breaker and Chicory, lined up for Winners Dog. Benny flapped his arms, like priming a pump, to dry the wet circles he had sweated onto his shirt.

Reginald called Chicory out first. His pleasure was almost palpable as he ran his hands over Chicory's head and body. He instructed Felix to move to the end of the ring and back so he could study his dog's movements. They were flawless. Regardless of Bess's desire for Breaker to win, she couldn't help feeling pride in this other puppy she had bred and seen born into the world.

Four other dogs went through their paces, and then it was Breaker's turn.

Bess held her breath and made a wish as Benny and Breaker stepped forward. As they approached the spot where Reginald was pointing, she was flooded with doubts.

Reginald wouldn't show her any favoritism, but now she began to imagine the other possibility — that he would be overly harsh.

Reginald took Breaker through his inspection and then ordered him around the ring. Only when he was in full motion could Reginald and the crowd at ringside appreciate the full extent of his fluid grace. Benny took Breaker through his paces flawlessly. No one could have done better. Reginald finished up with the remaining dogs and then called the whole class out again. They all went around one more time, and then he dismissed everyone except Breaker and Chicory and two others he told to wait on the side.

"The judge is making quick work of it," Bess heard someone behind her whisper.

"We'll see," replied her companion.

Beth held her breath. In a way, Breaker's whole future rested on the outcome. If he won this class, he had a chance of finishing in time. Otherwise, Westminster would be put off for another year — if ever.

Back and forth, Reginald went between McCreery's two puppies. Chicory had a body that wouldn't quit, but Breaker's face was pure Umpawaug. Bess's breath stuck in her throat when Reginald moved Chicory ahead of Breaker, but the contest wasn't over. Back Reginald came to give Breaker one last look. Bess could see he was tempted. He reached down and brushed his fingertips lightly over Breaker's downy topknot. It was something judges never do; he couldn't help himself.

Breaker closed his eyes and let out a sigh of poodle ecstasy that would bring a stone to life.

Reginald straightened up and pointed straight at Breaker. "First!"

⚜ ⚜ ⚜

"Look here," Sonya said, holding out a plastic bottle of pills. "I found them hidden under Benny's bed."

Benny's father turned the bottle slowly in his hands, as if a magician's trick could make the contents disappear. The glue from the missing prescription label stuck to the tips of his fingers. He dropped the bottle and rubbed his pant leg, as though the glue and not the pills could kill. "That's it! No more New Hope School. Dr. Kumar's had her last chance."

Sonya patted his arm. "Where else would he get poison like this? Not from anyone in this family, that's for sure."

He closed his eyes and breathed out a sigh. "And just when I thought we had a chance for Neusner & Neusner."

Chapter 44

"Pssst!"

David thought he heard a noise, but he must have imagined it. He had arrived at the school early to set up an obstacle course and hang the banner for the First Annual Field Day. He and Kate had planned it as a surprise for the students.

"Pssst!" came again.

He pushed aside a rhododendron branch and found Benny crouched frog-legged underneath. The ear flaps on his red-and-black cap must have itched on a pleasant fall morning, but the boy didn't seem to mind.

"Aren't you supposed to be in class?"

Benny looked around with narrowed eyes, making sure no one had spotted him. "Haven't you heard? My dad pulled me out of New Hope School. No more meetings with Dr. Kate, either."

"What happened?"

"Sonya found some pills in my secret hiding place, and my dad freaked. He thinks it's the school's fault."

David held his breath. "Are the pills yours?"

Benny jerked back. "No way, but thanks for asking. Sonya and my dad didn't bother."

David exhaled. "So whose are they?"

Benny zipped his lips shut with a clenched thumb

and forefinger.

David sighed. It must be someone important to him — maybe that strange girl he had a crush on, the one off in Europe someplace. "Does Kate know?"

Benny thrust out his lower lip belligerently. "She can't tell. She could get arrested if she did."

David didn't know much about the rules of confidentiality, but he was pretty sure that if Kate knew an underage child was on drugs, she would be obliged to tell his parents or even the authorities. "Maybe you should tell your dad the truth — if you want to stay in this school, that is."

Benny shook his head. "I can't. He's hired a tutor to come in every day. My dad says maybe now I'll finally get somewhere."

David looked at his watch. The students would be arriving soon. Worse yet, Benny's tutor could be looking for him.

Benny took the hint. "Here's my idea. Breaker only needs five more points to finish his championship. I've heard Bess bragging about this big show called Poodle Club of America. I'm pretty sure he could win it."

"A win at PCA would get anyone's attention, but what about your dad?"

"He'll get over it. He always does."

"Then ask Bess. She wouldn't miss PCA for the world." He turned to leave.

"Wait!" Benny called after him. "She'd like it a lot more if you asked." He held up his hands in prayer. "Puleeease."

The hunger in the boy's voice wrapped itself around David's heart, and he was tempted to give in. Then he remembered Kate's advice to let Benny speak for himself. "If you want to go badly enough, you'll find a way."

Benny sank onto the grass with his face cupped in his hands. The itch on the back of his neck went on almost a minute before he noticed. He reached up, expecting to shoo away a bug, and found McCreery sniffing him gently.

"What is it, big fella? Breaker needs PCA to get to Westminster, not you."

Benny thought he heard a low growl.

"You're right. It's a long shot for a puppy, but how else am I going to get on TV?"

The growl grew louder like Benny wasn't catching on. McCreery circled around in front and posed like he was standing for inspection.

Benny pushed himself up on one knee and leaned forward for a closer look. Yes, it was like he told Bess back when they thought Breaker's show days were over: McCreery was still one terrific looking poodle.

McCreery pawed Benny's arm impatiently and barked twice.

Not for the first time, Benny wished dogs could talk. Suddenly, his face lit up. "I get it. You want me to take you to Westminster!"

McCreery raised up on his hind legs and pressed his front paws against Benny's chest. He grinned into Benny's face and barked twice more.

"I'll do it!" Benny promised, almost without thinking. Bess had refused before, but this time he'd convince her. He'd do it for McCreery. A promise is a promise.

Chapter 45

Bess stretched out on the comfortable chaise lounge, the sun warming her through the French doors, but her mind was too full for sleep. A win at PCA was Breaker's best chance for an invitation to Westminster. He had two majors behind him and could pick up the remaining points at several smaller shows, but a dazzling finish at PCA would catch the invitation committee's eye. She could wait another year, but she had learned her lesson. She wasn't about to put off her dream again, not at her age. PCA was a chance she had to take, a million to one shot or not.

Still, she had a huge problem. She didn't have a handler. Benny was a natural and had done surprisingly well so far, but PCA was in a different league than he'd faced before. Jim Wren had his hands full with DandyGirl and DandyBoy, and Hannah would keep Felix hopping. She could hire a stranger, but the risk was even greater than with Benny. As she had discovered more than once, an Umpawaug poodle's feelings toward the handler were paramount.

A knock on the kitchen door startled her out of her reverie. Mona couldn't have forgotten her key again. She was tucked away upstairs, napping with McCreery. The two of them had become buddies during their trip to Boca Raton. She had even caught him sprawled across Mona's bed once or twice. With her in it!

Through the window, she spied Benny, his fist tight around a bunch of fall flowers she recognized from Mona's garden. She opened the door, and he thrust the bouquet at her. "For you."

She sniffed. "Very nice. Perhaps you'd better come in."

His eyes flicked to the cake waiting on the counter. It appeared to be three layers high and thick with creamy, yellow frosting.

"Mona made lemon ice box cake. Interested?"

"Sure. I'll put Breaker out so he doesn't go nuts begging." He held a treat over the dog's head and danced him out the door.

She sliced two big pieces and put the plates on opposite sides of the kitchen table. They both sat. He shoveled a large bite onto his fork and closed his eyes in pure delight as it slid down his throat. Apparently, he wasn't in any hurry to state the purpose of his visit while there was cake to be enjoyed.

Her impatience won out. "Oh, for heaven's sake. Are you here to discuss PCA or not?"

He rubbed a finger in his ear to get the ringing out. What was she up to? This was a new Bess he hadn't seen before. She used to look like she had a lot of gas, and now her face was all open and hopeful. He had read in one of the magazines in Dr. Kate's waiting room how constipation was the curse of old people because they didn't get out and exercise enough. He knew from his own experience it could make a person crabby. He wondered if she had tried that new medicine the ad on TV said everyone should ask their doctor about. Then he decided she was just excited about Breaker's new looks. He leaned forward, arms crossed on the table. "Tell me."

"Breaker has two majors but he still needs five more points for his championship. There are other ways to get them, but a win at PCA would finish him in one fell swoop."

He uncrossed his arms and leaned on his elbows. "I must be psychic. I was thinking the same thing!"

She pulled in her chin. "Breaker's a good-looking poodle, if I say so myself, but what are his chances? Nine hundred of the most beautiful poodles in the world will be there, and only one can win."

He smelled a rat. "You didn't mention Westminster."

"Westminster? Did you hear a word I said? He'd have to win PCA first."

He sat taller. "Yes, Westminster."

She crossed her arms. "Forget it. We're too late. The preparations for this year's show began days after the final toast was drunk to last year's winner."

He leaned back in his chair, unimpressed. "So, we shouldn't even try?"

She noticed a faint mustache was sprouting on his upper lip. For the first time, she felt like she was dealing with a young man who knew what he wanted and how to get it. She drew in a deep breath and blew out the answer. "All right, yes. If Breaker is invited, he can go."

He leaped to his feet, pumping his fist in the air, and shouted, "Yes, yes, yes!" He was so busy celebrating he missed a guilty look slither across her face.

She hadn't told him the whole truth. She was forced to give in to her better judgment and trust Benny at PCA, but Westminster was different. She had waited her whole life to make her dream come true. She still didn't know how she would find someone to help her, but it would happen — she hoped. Benny would earn glory enough if Breaker finished his championship at PCA.

"Anything else?" he asked, voice calm and steady again.

She looked up. For a moment, she had the fleeting thought that he, too, had a card hidden up his sleeve. "Not unless you have something to add."

He leaned forward, his expression determined. "I'll

take in Breaker at PCA, but only if we can take McCreery to Westminster, too."

Her mouth fell open and she started to object, but he held up a hand. "With his record, McCreery can get invited easy. He wants to go, trust me. Every time I practice with Breaker, he follows along." He lowered his voice confidentially. "I think he's jealous."

Her mouth opened and shut like a fish out of water. "Jealous? What's he got to be jealous about?"

His eyebrows flew up, a mirror imitation of hers. "You're kidding, right? You think he doesn't notice how you ignore him? All you think about is Breaker. What about McCreery?" He squirmed uncomfortably in his seat. "I could be jealous that McCreery picked you, but I'm not. I know he cares about me, and he knows I care about him."

She didn't answer for a long moment. He was talking about more than the dog. "I suppose you think a novice like you is ready for Westminster?" she asked finally.

"Sure," he answered, but his voice wavered a little. "I won Liberty Bell and I'll win PCA, too. You'll see."

She was back on firmer ground. "To compete at Westminster you've got to be exceptional. Not just the dog, the handler, too."

Benny puffed out his cheeks, ready to object, but she waved him into silence. She needed to think. The whole idea was crazy. Breaker and McCreery? Up against each other at Westminster? At McCreery's age, he didn't stand a chance. His time in the ring had passed, like hers. On the other hand, what harm would it do? No one would blame her if an unseasoned boy finished last with a dog whose sell-by date had passed. Besides, Benny had her over a barrel. If he didn't help her at PCA, Breaker would miss his chance. Still, she didn't want the boy to make a fool of himself. "I'll make you a deal. If you and Breaker win junior showmanship at PCA, you can take in McCreery at Westminster."

He wrinkled his nose like he had stepped in something nasty. "Junior showmanship? That's for babies."

She peered over her glasses. "Think again. Any kid can't just walk in with a dog at Westminster. It takes ten wins in open classes at official AKC shows to qualify. *You* wouldn't be eligible."

He thought it over. Tough as it would be for Breaker to win conformation at PCA, junior handlers would be tougher. The dog's looks didn't count, only his behavior. McCreery's whole future would depend on Breaker's manners. "How about I take McCreery instead? He could use the practice, don't you think?"

"Good try."

"Will McCreery and I be in the real class at Westminster — the same as Breaker?"

"If you win juniors at PCA."

His shoulders sagged. This was McCreery's only chance at Westminster, so what choice did he have? He was about to agree when he had an awful thought. She couldn't be that devious, could she?

He held up a hand. "Wait a minute. You said I couldn't enter junior showmanship at Westminster, but what about the regular show? Do they let kids do that?"

She gave him a dazzling smile. "They don't need a rule against it. They never imagined anybody would put their champion dog in the hands of a mere child against the world's most experienced handlers." She held out her hand. "Deal?"

He took a deep breath and started to shake, but at the last second, he jerked his hand back like it was on fire. "McCreery and Breaker would be in the ring at the same time. Even I can't do that. Maybe if you take that medicine on TV for your constipation, you could help out."

Truthfully, she had considered handling Breaker herself briefly, but her trick knee had been bothering her lately, and she couldn't chance it. She stretched her face into what she hoped was a convincing smile. "No problem, someone will come along."

Benny's lower lip quivered. "I've been Breaker's handler his whole life."

Bess lifted her chin. "Let's just concentrate on PCA."

He considered for a moment. "Will I still be on TV?"

The lie was tempting. "Not unless McCreery gets to compete in Group. He'll have to beat Breaker and the rest of the dogs to do that — not just poodles, the other non-sporting breeds, too. But they'll have streaming video on the website for the other classes. Anyone in the world with a computer can watch."

"No kidding? That's big."

She let his imagination fill in the details. Breaker was the boy's ticket to Westminster and vice versa. Benny would try his best, and so far, his best had been good enough.

Benny stood. "High five?"

"To Breaker," she called, slapping back.

McCreery, who had slipped downstairs and was eavesdropping, tapped Bess's foot impatiently with his paw. Perhaps he only wanted his dinner, perhaps something more. There was a glint in his eye she hadn't seen for years.

She pulled her eyebrows into a warning frown that encompassed the dog and the boy. "Let's not get ahead of ourselves. We've got to win PCA first."

Benny waved off the caution like a pesky fly. "No worry." He reached into his pocket and took out a dog treat. McCreery quivered in place, his eyes following every move. Benny laughed and slipped it into the dog's mouth. They were going to Westminster, he was certain of it, and Bess had done all the asking.

Mission accomplished, he rushed home and shut his bedroom door. For once, he couldn't wait to be alone. He shoved his math worksheet aside and opened the middle desk drawer. Buried under the scattered trading cards and old candy wrappers, he found the spiral notebook his mother had given him right after the divorce in case he wanted to write her a letter. Until now he hadn't anything to say that couldn't wait. The judge said he could see her every Wednesday after school and every other weekend, but what good was that when a mother was as busy as his? He was old enough to know whether a mother's a good mother or not, but the judge never asked him.

He ripped out a sheet, smoothing down the little tabs the round wires had made, and licked the point of his pencil:

Tuesday

Dear Mom,

Its me, Benny. How R U? I'm fine. Well, I am going to be in a really, really big dog show called P.C.A. Its short for Poodle Club of America. But don't get you're hopes up to high (like Dr. Kate says). Its really, really big. Bess says if we win I can go to West Minister (sp.!). The one on TV. Can you come? All the other moms will be there.

I love you.

XXXOOOXXX

Benny

(Your son)

P.S. Please try.

P.S.S. I can't wait.

Chapter 46

When Benny boasted that his Dad would let him go to PCA, he only half believed it himself, but now it was really happening. He had worked hard and done everything Sonya and the tutor asked. The article in the *Philadelphia Inquirer* helped, too. His dad launched into a big lecture on the benefits of sports and clean living, but Benny didn't mind that much because afterwards his dad said he could go.

Bess had warned Benny that junior handlers would be different, but he hadn't realized how strange it would actually seem until he lined up. All varieties and shades of poodles, including a few whose lineage was debatable, were mixed in together, and the handlers were as different as their dogs. The boy in front of him wearing a hand-me-down brown suit was handling a mid-sized white fluff ball with a perky bounce to her step. The boy's loose hold on the lead told Benny he knew what he was doing. Behind him, a skinny girl was trying to stack her white toy. The toy was trying to make friends with a dog that looked more Papillion than poodle handled by a tall boy with deep Latin eyes. A girl in green tights and a small brown dog rushed in last.

The judge entered the ring and passed her eyes quickly over Benny and the other young hopefuls waiting their turn.

He wondered how she would manage to decide among so many kids and dogs, but she immediately divided them into two lines according to age. He was in the second to oldest group in front of a short girl who practically had to drag her cream miniature to the end of the line. He was afraid the judge had put him in with a bunch of losers until she signaled a petite Chinese-American girl with the air of a star to stand in front of him with her perfectly turned-out black miniature. He didn't care how long the judge took to make up her mind. If it took forever, he was determined to win. Breaker seemed to sense how important the class was and followed every instruction perfectly.

Benny made the first cut, and the second, and then the judge told him to wait with the winners of the earlier classes. He overheard someone at ringside whisper that the tall girl wearing a gray pleated skirt and dark tights was last year's winner. In the old days, news like that would have turned his legs to cold spaghetti but no more.

At last, only the finalists were left in the ring, including Benny and Breaker. The judge called them out one by one. Benny couldn't help worrying about a long-legged girl wearing sparkly earrings whose cream standard poodle seemed to know what she was thinking ahead of time. Based on her looks, she would be too old for juniors next year.

Benny was last to be called. He snapped to attention as the judge told him, "Take your dog down to the end of the ring and back."

He straightened his tie, made sure his blue blazer was buttoned, and moved forward. "Okay, Breaker, let's give it our best shot," he said, and the two of them took off. Every handler and dog knew the contest was down to the wire, and the people watching in the stands sensed it, too. Not a sound could be heard. Then out of the silence, a booming voice shouted, "Go, Benny!"

A horrified gasp rippled through the spectators. He

recognized the voice and sensed the other junior handlers had turned to stare. He wanted to look, too, but this was his moment and he wasn't about to let anyone mess it up, not even his own mother.

"I'm in charge," he whispered, not making a single misstep.

"Way to go!" his mother's voice came again. His heart beat faster, and his palms began to sweat. The lead grew wet and slippery. He pushed down his growing panic.

"I'm in charge," he repeated. All the times Bess had made him take Breaker around an imaginary ring came back to him, and the familiarity of the task made his confidence return. Breaker added a little more spring to his step and held his head higher.

Just a few more steps and their turn would be over. Benny imagined how wonderful it would be when the judge handed him the trophy. He pictured his mother's big smile, and he smiled, too, letting his attention drift. A moment later, he came to with a start, certain he had ruined their chances, but all was well. With a rush of relief, he realized Breaker had covered for him and done exactly as they had practiced a hundred times.

The judge called out the girl in the gray pleated skirt for one more turn up and back, and Benny was afraid of what it might mean. Then the judge ordered the finalists to circle the ring a final time and line up near the judges' table.

Benny stifled an anxious yawn as the judge took one final look. He didn't understand why she was taking so long. Surely, she should have made up her mind by now. She turned her back and picked up something he couldn't see off the table. She turned again and held out a small silver trophy.

"First!" she called in a loud, clear voice and pointed at Benny and Breaker.

Breaker leaped high off the ground and planted a kiss on

Benny's face. Benny wiped it off with his sleeve and hugged Breaker back. He held the silver trophy high overhead for everyone in the stands to see and hurried out of the ring. He didn't even have time to show his prize up close to his mother. He only had finished the first part of his deal with Bess. If they had any possibility of a slot at Westminster this year, Breaker had to finish his championship today. It was their last chance.

Chapter 47

Breaker won! Benny and Breaker had won! Breaker was the best standard poodle in America, and they were going to Westminster. Bess could hardly believe it.

The day wasn't over yet. Tonight was the annual banquet when the election for next year's Best in Show judge would be held. It was an honor bestowed on the club's most knowledgeable and trusted members, a contest as full of intrigue and machinations as a presidential election. She was running against Hannah, and even a monsoon couldn't keep her away. Thank goodness Felix had offered to drop Benny off at his father's. The boy's excitement had practically done her in.

She was dressed and clipping on her best pearl earrings and matching choker when she heard a knock on the door.

"Hello, hello," Jim Wren called, poking his head through the open door. A room service waiter pushing a cart with a bottle of chilled champagne and hot hors d'oeuvres followed Holly and Jim inside. Breaker reached the company before Bess, skidding to a stop an inch short of toppling Holly over. Jim scrunched down on his haunches and stretched his arms toward Breaker who panted and cavorted like any ordinary dog and not the one just crowned best poodle in America. They made a handsome pair, smiling into each other's faces: Jim in his formal plaid bow tie, Breaker smelling like a wet wool sweater from nosing into the shower.

"Are you going to smooch with that dog all night or pour the champagne?" Bess pretended to grumble.

Jim popped the cork and passed glasses all around. "To Breaker."

"To Breaker," Bess repeated.

"Don't forget Benny," Holly added. "You've brought him along remarkably well, Bess."

"Hear, hear!" Jim said, raising the bottle and offering seconds. "Next stop Westminster."

Bess shifted uncomfortably. "I'm not sure," she said. She didn't know how to broach the question. Jim wasn't entering a dog in Westminster this year as far as she knew, but what if he were?

Jim caught Holly's eye and smiled behind his champagne flute. "DandyGirl still needs three more points to finish. I'm taking her to Amherst in a couple of weeks. How would you feel if I brought Breaker along? He obviously likes me, and it wouldn't hurt for him to get used to a different handler — in case you ever need one."

She fiddled with her choker. "That might be useful," she answered with no more emotion than if he had offered her salt for some hot buttered popcorn, but Jim's and Holly's smiles showed they weren't fooled. Jim would take in Breaker at Westminster. Problem solved.

As the door closed behind the friends, Breaker scooted out from under the coffee table. Thankfully, someone had remembered to leave the hors d'oeuvres out where he could help himself. He nibbled each one daintily, taking his time, and then padded over to the king-size bed. Nudging the pillows into a comfortable dog nest with his nose, he turned round and round in tight circles until he landed in the perfect spot. With a weighty sigh, America's top standard poodle closed his eyes and settled down for a quiet evening.

Bess made a good show of enjoying the awards banquet, but when the speeches were over and dessert was announced, she slipped out. The voting for Best in Show judge was about to begin, and she would need to absent herself in any case.

The cocktail lounge across from the banquet hall was empty and dark, except for the little lamps meant to look like candles on the round, wooden tables. Stale cigarette smoke hung in the air. She pulled out a captain's chair and sat. Her knee throbbed after the long day, so she stuck her leg up on the opposite chair and waited. Before long, someone would bring her the results.

As her eyes adjusted to the light, she noticed a tall figure in the shadows standing across from her. "Mind if I sit?"

Hannah was the last person she wanted to make chit-chat with, but she could hardly refuse. She waved at an empty chair. "Help yourself."

Hannah braced herself on the arms and eased down stiffly. She had worn herself out at the show and then finished the day campaigning for tonight's election. Bess would be amazed to know for whom, and Hannah hoped she would never find out. Bess had too much pride. "Congratulations on Breaker's win today," Hannah said. "Benny picked the right puppy."

Bess tipped her head to one side noncommittally.

Hannah twisted her large hands nervously, hoping Bess would ease her path. When she didn't, Hannah forged ahead. "We've been rivals a long time. For myself, I've enjoyed the competition. No one's done more for the breed than you, Bess. You've never compromised temperament for looks. The dogs I've loved most have had Umpawaug in back of them, and they will as long as I'm able. I wanted to say I hope you win tonight. You've earned it." When Bess didn't answer, she rose. "I'm sorry I intruded."

Bess's hand fluttered out, but the words stuck inside. If she didn't speak now, a door would close forever. "You'll get the face right eventually," she said with a half-smile. "Don't stop trying."

If they had more to say to each other, it was too late because Jim was coming through the door, holding up the judge's book for them to see. It was the equivalent of white smoke for the pope's selection. "We couldn't decide. Hannah, your turn's coming in two years. Bess, you're up next. Congratulations to you both."

Hannah stuck out her hand, and Bess grasped it. A sly smile spread across her face. "They probably think I'm going to die first," she said.

⚜ ⚜ ⚜

Sonya pushed the newspaper to one side and placed a plate of broiled salmon and asparagus spears in front of Benny's dad.

His expression was painful, as if he weren't about to enjoy one of his favorite dinners. "I've made a terrible mistake, Sonya. The pills we found in Benny's room belonged to his mother."

His wife's hand flew to her mouth. "No!"

"David Rutledge, the man Benny's always going on about, tipped me off. He said Benny's mother acted like she was on something at the big dog show and nearly ruined the boy's chances."

She eased into a chair. "No!" she repeated.

He went on as if she hadn't spoken. "Benny admitted pilfering her purse so she couldn't take the pills. They weren't even her prescription. She lied and told the doctor Benny needed them."

"That's horrible," she said, not quite hiding her "I-told-you-so" satisfaction.

"I've offered to pay for his mother's rehab. It's the least I can do for the boy."

She gasped. "And New Hope School?"

"Of course, and Dr. Kate, too." He pushed his plate to one side. "It's time I got to know my son better. Brains aren't everything in this world." He picked up the newspaper lying by his elbow and found the page he was looking for. He folded it back and tapped the spot with his finger. "See, right here: 'Boy Wins at Poodle Specialty Show.'"

"Oh, my," she murmured, grabbing the paper.

"Sports section, but still, the Sunday *New York Times*!" He reached in his pocket for a handkerchief and blew. "Who'd have thunk it? A son of mine."

She dropped the newspaper and came around to put her hands on his shoulders.

"You know, Sonya, I feel ashamed. All this time I've been wanting Benny to be someone he isn't, someone like me, if I'm honest." He sighed and studied his reflection in the matching metal salt and pepper shakers, as though seeing a memory and not his own face. "I remember the first time I saw my little son, back in the hospital when the nurse handed him to me. There wasn't that much of him to see, all swallowed up by that big towel or whatever they had him wrapped up in, wearing that funny little white cap." He splayed his fingers in front of him, turning his hand back and forth, assessing. "His little button nose was smaller than my pinkie nail."

He sighed and rested his hand on his heart. "I looked into the future and saw my boy following in my footsteps — me helping him every step of the way. He'd grow up to be the best part of me, the part that would last after I'm gone." He choked and dropped his chin, staring down at his open, empty hands. He pushed back his chair and stood, rubbing his hands against his sides. Sonya came around to stand beside him, waiting. He started to speak, then hesitated again, a man considering one last time if he could part with a favorite family heirloom.

"Fantasies are all well and good, but reality isn't so bad, either," he said finally. "It's time I faced up to the fact that not everyone's cut out to be a partner in a law firm or even a college man. There are other talents in this world just as important, and I think my son has found his."

She bobbed her head and smiled encouragingly. "And he's only a teenager!"

Chapter 48

Benny couldn't believe his eyes. Steffie was on the bench in front of the school waiting for him. She had been gone for months, ever since her parents had pulled her out of summer school and flown her off to Europe. He was eager to tell her the truth about the pills, but his mind was elsewhere at the moment. Underneath her camel hair coat, she was wearing trendy denim jeans and a yellow collared shirt. He wondered if her glossy pink lipstick would taste like cherry if she let him kiss her.

"What happened? Your clothes?"

She turned up her face, blinking rapidly. "I bought them myself. How do I look?"

He had a fleeting thought she might be flirting with him and tucked in his stomach. "You look great. Just like a normal kid." His hand flew to his mouth. "Oops, sorry. Maybe I'm catching Asperger's, too."

She smiled. "I don't think it's something you can catch." Her voice was soft, without a hint of anger. "I gave my mother strict instructions to stop shopping for me. I've got my own style now, and she's not going to change me."

"That's terrific," he said and felt heat rising in his cheeks.

She scooted over to make space beside her. "I'm sorry, too, for the mean things I said about the school. I finally figured out how special New Hope School really is. Smart kids can be dumb sometimes."

They peeked at each other out of the corner of their eyes and grinned. "Maybe," he said, "but I'd lots rather be smart like you. Sometimes my head hurts from trying to figure stuff out, and I can't keep my body still. It drives Sonya crazy, but lately she seems to be chilling a bit."

"Really?" she asked distractedly.

"I think it's because of my dad. Now that he's not so worried about me, she isn't so worried about him. She really loves him." He dropped his eyes. "Not like my mom."

She leaned closer. "I'm really proud of the way you've become a famous handler. Not many kids our age even know what they want to be, and you have a successful career already. Pretty smart, huh?"

He squirmed with adolescent embarrassment. "I guess you're right."

She cleared her throat. The corners of her mouth were pulled down like Dr. Kate's when she was worried. "I've got some news of my own."

He held his breath. From her tone of voice, he was pretty sure he wouldn't like it.

She straightened up, bracing herself. "I might as well just say it. I'm leaving New Hope School."

He exhaled, relieved it wasn't worse. "Yeah, sure. You're a brain. You're heading for Barlow High next year."

She tried a smile, but it trembled on her lips. "No, not there, and I mean right away. I only came today so I could tell you myself."

He jumped to his feet. He had never imagined anything this terrible. "You can't. You just got back."

She shrugged. "I'm used to changing schools by now. Besides, Oakwood Friends won't be so bad."

He wasn't buying it. "You're my best friend. Who can I talk to when you're gone?"

"Poughkeepsie isn't that far. I'll be back on school vacations. Besides, you've got plenty of people to talk to right here: Adam, Dr. Kate, David, your dad." She tried again for a smile.

His leg bounced up and down like a paddleball on a rubber string. "Yeah, but none of them are you."

She stood in front of him and laid a hand on his arm. He felt tingly all over and his leg jiggled faster.

"Sorry," he apologized. "Girls get to me sometimes, especially pretty ones. It gives me thoughts in bed at night, but Dr. Kate says not to worry. It's normal."

She dropped her eyes. "Yeah, Dr. Kate talked to me, too. I've decided I'm not going to have sex after all, not for a long, long time."

"That's good," Benny said. "I mean, I guess it is. Just don't forget about me, okay?"

"I'll never forget you, Benny." She said it like a promise.

"Me, neither," he said, examining his hightops.

"My mother's given up on her Asperger's kick, and I'm never going to let anyone tell me there's something wrong with me again."

"That's great, Steffie." He really meant it, even though his heart was breaking.

She studied his face as if she was trying to engrave it into her memory forever. "I'm sure I'll make lots of new friends at Oakwood but none of them will be as special as you, Benny."

His hightops were toe to toe with her penny loafers. A rosy blotch colored his neck and spread until his cheeks were bright red. "I've heard a person never forgets his first kiss. Not that this would be my first," he added, hastening to cover his mistake.

"Whatever. It sounds like a good idea."

He leaned, and she leaned, and as their lips touched,

Dr. Kate happened to look out the window.

"Asperger's? That's a good one," she said disgustedly and hurried downstairs to tell Steffie good-bye.

⚜ ⚜ ⚜

"You heard me," Benny's dad told Sonya. "His mother's suing for custody. Now that Benny's in the newspaper, she thinks he's going to be rich."

Sonya handed a steaming cup mulled cider to her husband. "She can't be serious. A silver trophy or two won't pay the bills."

Benny's dad took a deep swallow before answering. "She's got some shrink to say she's off the pills, and she's hired a shyster lawyer. The worst part is the judge is bound to ask Benny who he wants to live with. He's old enough now."

"Do you really think he'd choose that woman after everything she's done?"

His eyebrows lifted in surprise. Were those tears glistening in her eyes? For once, she sounded more concerned for Benny than hateful toward his mother. She and Benny had been spending more time enjoying each other's company and less arguing over his diet. Just last night he had come home to find them giggling and high-fiving when the guy got the girl at the end of one of Sonya's chick flicks, and she was the one who had asked whether they could all take a trip together next summer to a place Benny would enjoy. Was Sonya finally growing fond of his son? Did Benny feel it, too? Not that he expected or even wanted Benny's feelings for his mother to change. He only hoped his son would have the maturity to choose what was best for him on his day in court.

He sighed and placed the empty cup carelessly on its saucer. It teetered back and forth before toppling on its side with a jarring note of finality. He reached for Sonya's hand and answered huskily. "She's his mother. He'll never stop wanting her."

Chapter 49

Benny plopped down on Dr. Kate's couch. "You know how you're always telling me to keep my feet on the ground and not get my hopes up? Well, you're not as smart as you think. I always hoped my mom would fight for custody of me, and now she's doing it."

Kate's blood ran cold. Benny's dad had warned her his mother might do this, and now she had. Kate wasn't sure Benny had the maturity to handle the choice the lawyers would put in front of him.

She drew in a deep breath. "Both your parents want you. The question is what do you want?"

He pushed back his bangs and grinned broadly. "I want," he said and stopped. "I want," he began again. Then he dropped the mask, and his eyes flooded with tears. "I want to live with them both. Sonya, too."

A lump formed in her throat. She swallowed it down. "Benny, you know that's not possible."

He rolled onto his back, staring at the ceiling as if the solution were written there. "My mom said she'd let me have a dog, any kind I want. A real dog, not a poodle."

"Is that your opinion or hers?"

He pushed himself up and sat. "I told her a poodle is a real dog, but she said I'd look better on TV with another kind. Maybe a Pomeranian."

"So she's thinking about TV, not you or the dog?"

He stuck out his chin and didn't answer.

Kate drew in a deep breath and tried to calm her racing heart. "What about McCreery? And Breaker? Aren't they counting on you?"

He dropped his chin onto his chest. "My mom got all excited when I won PCA. I told her I'd done it for her, but that wasn't the whole story."

"What was?"

He stood and swung his arms back and forth in an arc. "I did it for me," he said finally. "For once in my life, I found something I could do better than the other kids. It felt great."

She held his eyes. "Are you willing to give that up? For anyone?"

He wrinkled his brow, and she could tell he was thinking harder than he ever had before in his life. She held her breath, hoping for the answer that would free him.

After a moment, it came. He spun in place on one leg and grinned. He had made the right choice. He had chosen for him.

His face grew serious again. "You know, I think I'm beginning to understand my mother better. I used to want to make her happy more than anything in the world — except maybe a dog — but now I see what you mean when you say she's never going to change. She nodded, reluctant to derail his thinking.

"Lately, I've been wishing for something different I want."

"Oh? What's that?"

"To have my whole family all together and happy — me, my mom, my dad, even Sonya. We'd laugh and have a good time, everybody getting along. Maybe they'd say they were proud of me, and I'd tell them how much I love them all." He stood and sighed, his head bowed, but then his voice grew stronger. "I don't mean forever. I know that can't happen. But if it could come true just once, even for one night, I'd make the memory last my whole life."

She swallowed hard and stood, too. Her hands fluttered at her sides, as though they wanted to hug him. "That's a beautiful thought, Benny. Thanks for sharing it with me."

He reached for the homework paper he had left lying on the couch and tucked it into his jacket pocket. He smiled, shoulders relaxed. "I'd better get going. Sonya's making steak and baked potatoes for dinner, my favorite, and I don't want to be late."

⚜⚜⚜

Sonya's mouth tilted in a skeptical smile. "Benny says the old lady next door is bringing two poodles to Westminster, and he's going to take one into the show ring himself."

Benny's dad cut a generous slice of Boston cream pie and slid it onto a clean plate. A proud smile played on his lips. "He's earned it. Dogs can't just turn up for a big show like that. They have to qualify."

"No wonder he's been so jumpy. More than usual, I mean. I thought once the custody hearing was over, he'd settle down again."

He scooped some custard off the edge of the knife with his finger and popped it in his mouth. "I can hardly believe it's over myself. Thank goodness the judge didn't try to make him pick her or us, but she had to be swayed by how much he loves his school and the fact that we sent him there. Of course, he still gets to visit his mother whenever he wants." He picked up the plate and headed upstairs to where his son was finishing his homework.

"Should I buy tickets?" Sonya called after him.

He waved a big hand over his head. "Do bears sleep in the woods? Get a few extra. I'll pass them out to my partners."

Chapter 50

Bess inhaled the aroma of freshly baked oatmeal raisin cookies and saw in a panic that Mona had left them unguarded on the kitchen counter. She stuck one in her pocket, scooped the rest onto a plate and shoved them in a cabinet with a sigh of relief. If Breaker hadn't been at Jim's so they could practice together, he would have devoured every one. Not that McCreery was an angel. Now that she thought about it, where was he? Then she remembered. Benny had dropped by earlier and said he would give his pal some exercise. He had no idea she was about to shatter his happiness.

She peeked out the window. Sure enough, Benny was heading into the puppy shed with McCreery, but why? There was nothing of interest inside. Benny was smiling and McCreery was wagging his tail excitedly. She tossed the uneaten cookie into the sink, turned on the disposal, and shrugged into her pea jacket.

She opened the puppy shed door and gasped. McCreery was standing patiently on the grooming table. Benny was aiming the clippers straight for his hindquarters.

She rushed inside. "Benny, stop! One mistake and it'll take months to grow out."

He didn't look up. "It can't be that hard. I've seen you do it plenty of times."

She spoke quickly. "Well, it is. You shouldn't be fooling around like that."

He wheeled around, lips tight. "Somebody's got to do it. You're not."

She held out her hand, hoping it would stay steady, and motioned for the clippers. "Please."

He looked back at McCreery, hesitated, and then pulled the cord from the wall. His wrist showed where he had outgrown his shirt sleeve. The clippers clattered to the floor.

She gestured toward the milking stool. It hadn't been used since Breaker and the others were tiny puppies. "Sit, please. You need to listen."

He considered for a minute and then perched himself next to McCreery on the grooming table. He circled the dog's neck with his arm. "You registered him, didn't you? He can go?"

She sat on the stool, leaning forward, hands clasped. "Yes, I registered him, but he can't go."

He bolted to his feet, his hands balled into fists. "You're nothing but a rotten, stinking liar. You've been stringing me along all this time for your precious Breaker."

A tight band squeezed her skull. When she had promised the boy, the odds against him were overwhelming. The idea that he and Breaker could win junior showmanship at a big event like PCA seemed ludicrous, not to mention beating all those other standard poodles.

She sucked in a deep breath. "McCreery is ten years old, Benny. In his day, he was the greatest of them all, but he's had his turn. It's time for the next generation."

"You're old. I don't see you giving up." He flung the words, past caring whether he hurt her or not. "You might try thinking about someone besides yourself once in a while. What about McCreery's feelings?"

She held his gaze, willing herself not to let the hurt

show. "You don't understand," she answered calmly. "I *am* thinking about McCreery. A few years ago, a seven-year-old German shepherd won at Westminster, but mostly the winners are youngsters. Do you want people calling him an old has-been?"

He jumped down. "It's not fair. McCreery's loved you all his life, and you've never given him a chance. He's waited and waited, hoping his time would come, and all you do is ignore him."

She looked from boy to dog to boy again. He was talking about more than the dog. "It means that much to you?"

He nodded, tears threatening.

She stood and began pacing. "Even if I change my mind, McCreery's not in show coat. That's not allowed."

Benny reached behind him and held up a book with a faded green cover. *Poodles in America* was written on the spine. The gold embossed letters were flaking with age and use. "I found this in a cabinet. The dogs have lots of funny-looking clips from the olden days. Maybe he could wear one of them."

Bess reached for the book. It fell open at a familiar page. Her finger traced the photo of a handsome dog in full coat. "Jester, McCreery's great-great-great-grandfather," she said softly, voice choking. On the opposite page, a youthful Hannah Washington was holding a silver cup beside a white poodle.

Benny paced impatiently. He was interested in today, not something that happened a hundred years ago. "So? What do you think? Could McCreery get into Westminster with one of those crazy clips?"

She flipped through the pages, considering. "I guess he could appear in a hunting clip," she said finally. "The technical name is the historically correct continental — HCC."

Benny pumped his arm. "Yes!"

She looked at the boy's eager face, mirroring the naïve hopes she had felt with her first puppy, decades before Benny was born. She tossed the book back onto the counter. "I'm sorry. I've let you get your hopes up for nothing. Even with the right clip, McCreery wouldn't stand a chance."

Benny clenched his fists, trying to slow his breath. "Who cares if he wins? It's the dream that matters. Remember?"

She shut her eyes. Her head swung back and forth in small, rapid movements like a wind-up toy. She felt off balance, like he was the adult and she was the child. Had she really forgotten? Was Westminster only a dream for the imagination of youth, a fairy tale whose ending had become stale in the re-telling, or was she meant to grab this one final chance with both hands whatever the outcome?

She heard him open the door. She raised her eyes. "Wait! We'll do it. We'll take them both."

Benny turned and grinned, showing every one of the metal spikes on his braces.

She hesitated, then held up her hand. "High five?"

He laughed out loud and smacked back. "Don't worry. You won't be sorry."

Strange, she almost believed it herself.

Chapter 51

Mona found Bess in the puppy shed up to her elbows in soapsuds. A wet poodle in a round metal tub looked up at her blinky-eyed. "I stopped by to wish you luck tomorrow. Westminster, at last!" She sighed, like she was the one who had been waiting all these years. She slipped off her coat, as if she planned to stay awhile, and stepped closer to the sopping-wet dog. "He looks splendid," she said.

Bess brushed her bangs out of her eyes with her arm. "He doesn't look his age, that's for sure."

Mona's eyes widened. She hadn't realized the dog in the tub was McCreery. "Don't tell me you're taking McCreery to Westminster."

Bess replaced the cap on the bottle of her special crème shampoo with just a hint of lavender for luck. "All right, I won't if it makes you feel better."

Mona tossed her head and sniffed. "I hope you know what you're doing. That dog has feelings, you know." She straightened the waistband on the emerald green sweater she had swapped with Bess two Christmases ago. It was her favorite.

Bess wiped some stray bubbles off her cheek with the back of her hand. "You won't believe me, but he wants to go so badly he can taste it."

Mona did believe her, and it was an odd sensation. "Does

that mean Breaker and McCreery will be competing against each other?"

"First time ever for a father and son combination at Westminster," Bess answered, unable to hide her pride.

Mona studied her manicure, digesting the news. She had tried one of those new metallic blue colors, Midnight Passion. "So what happens if one of them wins Best Poodle?" she asked, satisfied her nails were perfect and the latest thing.

Bess turned the water on full force, spraying droplets over Mona's red suede shoes. "It'll never happen."

Mona stuck out her lip. "But if it does?"

"Then he'll have to beat all the other winners of all the other breeds in Non-Sporting."

"And if he wins Non-Sporting?"

"Then he'll have to beat the winners of the other six Groups — Working Dogs, Hounds, Sporting, Herding, Terriers, and Toys, the winners of twenty-five hundred champion dogs. Think of the odds."

Mona was impressed. "And that's it? He'll win Westminster?"

"Stop! Breaker's good-looking, but he's still a puppy. Only dogs with records a mile long ever win Best in Show."

"Like McCreery," Mona said, folding her arms triumphantly.

"McCreery? In the world of show dogs, he's ancient. A living relic — like us."

Mona looked again. She could have sworn McCreery winked, but it must have been a drop of shampoo in his eye. "That's not what he thinks."

Bess stepped around in front and saw it, too. McCreery's old sparkle shone through, soaking wet coat and all. Bess reached for a towel and invited him to hop out of the tub. Both sisters stood back while he shook off the worst of the water.

"I have to agree with you, Mona," Bess conceded, adding to a conversation full of surprises. "McCreery hasn't looked this good in years. That treadmill has really gotten him in shape."

"Treadmill? You don't mean you've been making that poor dog work out on a treadmill?"

"Don't be ridiculous," Bess snorted. "Do you think I'd make a dog of mine do something he didn't want? The doctor said it'd be good for my knee, and McCreery hopped aboard one afternoon when I turned it on. It's done wonders for us both."

Mona shrugged back into her Chesterfield. "All I can say is that poodle has a strange look in his eye. There's no telling what he might have in store for you tomorrow."

Funny, Bess was thinking the same thing herself.

Chapter 52

Hands on his hips, head thrust back, Benny gulped in deep breaths like he had just finished an Olympic weightlifting event. An empty dog crate with a bag of liver treats taped on top hung precariously off the back of the Country Squire. Off to the side, McCreery waited, his whole body quivering with anticipation. Benny pushed the crate the rest of the way in with his shoulder, and McCreery leaped inside without an invitation. He lay down with an air of calm expectancy, as if a few more hours wouldn't matter after a lifetime of waiting.

Benny bent over at the waist and massaged his back. "Where's David? He promised he'd help me load the car."

Bess looked up from the map David had drawn of their route to Madison Square Garden and studied Benny carefully, as if he was on exhibit himself. In the ambient light from the car headlights, she saw a sharp crease in his gray pants, and his dress shoes boasted a fresh shine. A blue-and-red striped tie and a starched white collar were visible through the gap in his trench coat. His blue blazer would be underneath. The familiar checkered cap topped the outfit. If she didn't keep an eye on him, he would wear it in the show ring.

As for herself, she always dressed to the nines for a big show. A silk man-tailored shirt, perfectly ironed, was covered by her signature red jacket so her friends would have no trouble finding her. Not a spot was on it. A heavy gold chain and matching earrings were *de rigueur* for such an occasion; her fingers were unadorned. She had almost switched her usual black pants for a skirt, but decided against it. Too much like Mona.

She opened the collar of her camel hair coat and unfastened her mother's old-fashioned watch pin. She held it up to her ear and shook it. The ticking was plainly audible. The hands read a few minutes to six a.m. She stood on tiptoes and peered through the trees. A soft glow was visible behind the drawn curtains of David's cottage. "Stay here. I'll see what's keeping David."

She expected her son would meet her halfway, but she made it to the front stoop first. Even then, she had to knock a couple of times before he opened the door. He was wearing a striped bathrobe. A pair of blue pajama legs showed at the bottom.

"Why aren't you ready? Are you sick?" She tried peering behind him, but he kept his shoulder in place.

He took a deep breath. "I'm sorry as I can be, but I can't go with you today. Lotus hasn't been herself all night, so Kate brought her here." He leaned into her confidentially. "She thinks I inherited some knowledge of dogs from you."

She gave a skeptical cough and waited for him to go on.

He straightened up. "I don't think it's serious. The poor little thing probably ate something that didn't agree with her, maybe the anchovies in the Caesar salad, but Kate can't miss school today, and someone needs to stay with Lotus"

She bit back the words on the tip of her tongue. This was the biggest show of her life. Mona was planning to watch on TV — if one of the dogs made it that far — but she thought her son would be there with her.

"You feed that dog too much junk. She's getting pudgy,"

was all she said. She would never admit how disappointed she felt.

He pulled his sash tighter against the cold morning air. "Kate has some medicine left over from Lotus's appointment with the vet last month. Her symptoms are pretty much the same. She'll be all right."

She stretched her neck, still trying to peek inside. "Sure I can't help?"

"Thanks, anyway. We've got it under control. If not, Dr. Hammer's close by."

She narrowed her eyes. He had a secretive look about him she recognized from his childhood. There was more to his change of plans than he was admitting. What was hidden behind the door he was blocking with his shoulder? She peeked under his arm and saw a pair of women's shoes lying on the floor. They were the open-back style Kate preferred even in winter. Maybe Kate had embraced her advice after all and taken a chance. She swallowed the smile that threatened to spill out. If more had developed between Kate and her son than they wanted to announce, she needed to keep her hopes to herself. But with her whole heart, she wanted it to be true.

He took her elbow and guided her down the front steps. "You'll be fine. Benny, too. Holly and Jim will be there, and everyone here will be rooting for you each step of the way."

"She pulled up her coat collar. "You're right," she said. She no longer minded that he wouldn't be with her today. Westminster was her dream; it had never been his. Lotus was Kate's dog, and he belonged with her now.

David watched until he heard the car engine turn over. Then he closed the door gently. Waiting a minute for his eyes to adjust to the soft light from the pot-bellied stove, he tiptoed over to the big easy chair in the corner. He leaned down and kissed the top of Kate's head. She smiled in her sleep and snuggled deeper into the blanket he had thrown over her in the early hours of the morning.

Stepping softly, he moved behind her chair. His attention was on the old wicker laundry basket Bess had used in the past for newborn puppies. He knelt down and listened carefully. Lotus's soft snores drifted up. Pulling back the old towel he had draped over the handle to keep out a draft, he peeked. Yes, there they were: one, two, three, four. All alive, breathing softly. He leaned back on his haunches and indulged in a contented chuckle. McCreery's latest offspring!

Some people might disagree, but he thought his mother would be rather pleased once she got over the initial shock. After all, there was a whole school full of children who would want a puppy to take home. It was just bad luck the puppies had chosen today to get born. He would have liked his mother to see them right away, but it wouldn't be fair to distract her with newborns on the biggest day of her show career.

He cocked his head. What was that? He thought he heard a high-pitched squeak, so soft and quick he might not have heard it at all. There it was again. He pulled the towel back a smidgen to let in a little light. Yes, it was him all right: the brown boy with the big round belly, the one with his father's unmistakable Umpawaug nose. Even in his first sleep, he was using his sturdy hind legs to push his siblings out of the way.

He leaned in and stroked Lotus's crown with one finger. "You've done well, little mama. Half Umpawaug, half New Hope School — an almost perfect combination."

Chapter 53

Benny and Bess rode mostly in silence, too nervous for chitchat. Benny read out loud from the map, and two hours later they made their turn safely onto 34th Street. Madison Square Garden, straight ahead! Colorful purple and gold spotlights swooped back and forth in the morning sky, announcing that America's First Dog would be chosen tonight. A New York City traffic cop with a whistle in his mouth waved white-gloved hands in choreographed movements. He pointed at their car and blew. A string of greyhounds and a chunky bulldog ambled across the busy street in front of them. The whistle blew again, and they pulled up at the unloading dock.

Benny led the way to the grooming area downstairs, holding McCreery's lead. He never knew there could be so many kinds of dogs in one place. Twenty-five hundred dogs of every imaginable size, shape, and color were squeezed in together. Spilling out into the narrow aisles, anxious handlers brushed and teased like Fifth Avenue hairdressers prepping runway models.

He nodded over the top of his load toward the roped-off area meant for the dogs' restroom. "The place doesn't even smell like dog," he said, but Bess was too busy pretending it was all old hat to reply. She just cocked an eyebrow at McCreery who was sniffing the floor for all the delicious dog aromas he could smell even if Benny couldn't.

Benny looked from side to side hoping to spot Breaker first, but the dog's sharp eyes beat him to it. The puppy wriggled excitedly on the grooming table where Jim was completing a last minute comb-out. Benny knew better than to touch Breaker's coat, but he patted his muzzle where it wouldn't do any damage.

"Breaker looks good, Jim. You've done a great job," Bess said, her pride hanging out like a Fourth of July flag.

Jim hid a pleased smile. "I'd say Breaker's got a decent chance today, but he's got some stiff competition."

Benny squinted and thought he spotted Hannah's tall figure off to the right. Breaker had beaten Chicory at Liberty Bell and PCA, but Chicory had won the first time the two brothers went up against each other at Quinnipiac. Felix would be taking Chicory into the ring tonight, and Felix was one of the best.

"Fandango's here, too, of course," Jim continued. "He's probably been sedated up to his eyeballs after the way he snapped at his handler at Liberty Bell."

Benny looked down the crowded aisle to where Jim was pointing. Fandango's striking white coat was easy to spot. He swallowed nervously, knowing that the handsome dog had almost equaled his sire's record already. A win tonight would put him over the top. He screwed his face into a frown. "You mean drugs?"

"Desperate handlers have been driven to it," Jim admitted.

"Not me, not even for Westminster," Benny said. "Too many people can get hurt."

A trio of black standard poodles moved quickly past them. Bess turned to Jim, a puzzled look on her face. "For a moment, I thought one of those dogs was DandyLady, but that's impossible. You retired her three years ago after she went Best of Opposite Sex here. She's probably sleeping on your bed at home."

"The best dog you ever sold us. We've loved having her, penchant for bathing in mud puddles and all."

Jim checked Breaker a final time and invited him down off the table. Breaker shook out his coat, his tail whirring back and forth excitedly. He was still in a puppy cut, but his rich, chestnut coat was coming in nicely. Jim had scissored his growing mane the best he could. Usually, dogs Breaker's age would be at home growing more coat to create the poodle's dramatic appearance, but what Breaker lacked in the showiness of a full coat, he made up for in the sparkle coming from inside. A poodle his age had never looked better, and he knew it. The glint in his eye fairly shouted "Step aside, boys. I'm here."

Benny looked back and forth between Breaker and McCreery, father and son. McCreery was in top form himself. The historic continental clip suited him. His coat had enough gray mixed in to create a soft, warm undertone and conveyed an innate dignity and strength of character that came with age. Benny rested his hands on his stomach and pronounced confidently, "I think McCreery has a good chance, too."

McCreery's patience stretched only so thin, and he nudged Bess's arm. She tapped the grooming table with a metal comb and signaled him on board. "Feel like a snack while I'm finishing up?" she asked Benny. "There's a row of concession stands along the far wall. You've got plenty of time."

He patted his stomach. The baby fat was almost gone. "Are you kidding? I couldn't swallow if my life depended on it."

After what seemed like an interminable wait, it was time for standard poodles dogs. Jim stuck out his hand and said, "Good luck, son." Then he hurried upstairs with Breaker.

Benny picked up the armband with McCreery's number

and slid it up his arm. McCreery turned to look at him. They stared at each other deeply, as though reading each other's thoughts. Just like Benny's dog book said, some dogs and their people have special powers of communication. He and McCreery had proven it over and over, going back to when he had found McCreery sick and lying at the end of his dad's driveway.

He filled his lungs and eased the air out slowly like a leaky balloon. "This is it, big fella," he said and signaled McCreery forward. Bess fell in step alongside.

The noise rising from the crowd was so loud Benny thought half the people in New York must have come to watch. As they reached the portal to the stadium, his knees buckled slightly. McCreery looked back at him and tugged on the lead. No opening night jitters for this old champion; he was raring to go. It gave Benny the encouragement he needed. He straightened his tie, tucked in his stomach, and stepped inside.

Westminster Kennel Club! A tingling sensation traveled up McCreery's lead to the tips of Benny's fingers. He flexed them back and forth, reassured they were still working. The mundane smells of hot dogs and popcorn, human sweat, and dog breath mingled with the residues of hope and loss. For a minute, he thought he might sneeze. Instead, his eyes were drawn upward. Row upon row of seats rose up to the ceiling, the highest so far away he could barely make them out, all filled with people wondering who would be chosen the finest dog in America. Somewhere in that crowd, his father and Sonya were watching. He scanned the bleachers, knowing it would be a miracle if he could spot them.

A sudden flash of light caught his eye. A spotlight bounced off something shiny in the section for people who wanted the best view. He stopped, and McCreery stopped, too, wondering what could be holding them up. The dog didn't see what Benny saw: the distinguished man in a coat with a lambskin collar, the tall lady whose auburn hair fell in soft curls down her back. The flash came from a pin shaped like a lightning bolt that his dad had given Sonya in a blue box for her birthday. And then, unbelievably, he noticed a second woman sitting on his dad's other side. Straight, sandy hair, so like his own, hung down around her face like a mantilla.

His arm shot into the air in a victory salute. They came, the three of them together, just like in the wish he'd told Dr. Kate. He knew the happiness wouldn't last, that it was just for tonight, but for tonight life was almost perfect.

Bess tapped Benny's arm. He had forgotten she was there. She nodded to her right. A small cluster of reporters was gathered around Nancy Valentine dressed in a chartreuse silk suit. "The press love Nancy because she can give an interview in four languages," she whispered.

Benny recognized the CNN reporter with lots of hair holding the microphone. The man posed a serious expression and signaled the cameraman closer. "Ms. Valentine, what are your thoughts on the standard schnauzer? We hear he's the favorite."

Nancy smiled and flipped her elegant hands out to the side. "How could I judge something like that, if you'll pardon my little pun. Every dog here is a champion, literally, and they seem to get more beautiful every year." She knew what she was talking about. Last year, she had judged Westminster's Best in Show.

Nancy waved Bess and Benny over. He tugged on the cuffs of his blazer and brushed the bangs off his forehead. "You remember Bess Rutledge — Umpawaug Kennels?" Nancy asked the reporter.

He gave Bess a toothy grin. "Yeah, sure."

Nancy put her hand on Benny's shoulder. "Here's the man you should be interviewing. Benny is taking in the senior half of the only father-son combination in

Westminster history. Bess is the breeder-owner."

The reporter switched off the microphone and ordered the cameraman, "Get some footage of the kid with the old dog. I'll try to get it on the ten o'clock news," he promised Nancy before moving on.

Nancy dabbed at her forehead, only half-feigning exhaustion, and turned to Bess. "There's lots of interest in the poodles this year. Fandango's drawing a lot of attention, and everyone's noticed Breaker's credentials, but wait until they see McCreery."

Benny's face lit up like a Broadway marquee. "I told you."

Bess avoided his eyes. Meeting those reporters, listening to Nancy, brought back her misgivings. She was taking a risk exposing the old champion's reputation to that kind of scrutiny.

Nancy misunderstood the doubts playing on Bess's face. She assumed they were about Benny. "If you took in McCreery yourself, you'd be the sentimental favorite. The judge would almost have to make it easy on herself and give you the win."

Benny felt heat rising up through his whole body. Everything he had worked for all these months gone in a word? He sucked in a deep breath, fingers curled into a fist, and then, remembering himself, sighed it out slowly. He looked Bess in the eye. "Take Breaker. I'm the one who believes in McCreery, not you."

Bess turned to Nancy. "Benny's right. If it weren't for him — and my son David — I wouldn't be here. I know you mean well, but Benny's earned his chance. He'll take in McCreery."

Nancy watched the old woman, the boy, and the old dog stride determinedly toward the ring for standard poodles. She shook her head and said to herself, "Wait till Animal Planet gets a hold of that story."

Chapter 54

Bess found her seat between Holly and Nancy and opened the show catalogue to the section on standard poodles. She ran her finger down the pages, studying the dogs' parents and kennels. She peered over the top of her glasses at Nancy. "Have you noticed how many of McCreery's get are entered this year?" She flipped a couple of pages. "In fact, a whole slew of Umpawaug-bred poodles are on the premises."

"Mmm," Holly murmured. She pointed. "Here they come."

Twenty standard poodles lined up outside the ring. Fandango was at the head of the line and next came Chicory. Breaker and McCreery were at the end of the line. The judge called the class into the ring and ran everyone around twice before he divided them into two lines.

"McCreery's never looked better, Bess. If you ask me, he's a finer dog now than all those years ago at PCA," Nancy said.

The judge took his time examining each dog carefully. With each passing minute, the little tension knot in Bess's neck grew tighter. The longer the judge took, the harder it would be for Benny to hold himself together, not to mention the wear and tear on McCreery. The dog was no spring chicken, in spite of how well he had gotten himself up for today.

After what seemed a lifetime, the judge joined the two halves together and told them to circle the ring. As the dogs passed by, he checked their numbers against notes he had written on a piece of paper and signaled some of them to one side. Chicory came out, then Fandango, then Breaker. A black dog Bess had sold as a puppy to his handler was next, followed by a silver and two other blacks she didn't know.

"I'm pretty sure Breaker's in the line he's planning to keep," Holly said.

"Don't count chickens," Bess warned, afraid to hope.

The judge studied the two lines carefully one more time. It seemed as though Breaker had made the cut. The judge started to walk away, then, almost as an afterthought, turned and pointed at McCreery.

The people in the grandstands began studying his pedigree in their catalogues. "That's who he is," the woman sitting behind Bess told her companion.

Bess held her breath. Could Breaker and McCreery both have made the short list? In answer to her silent question, the judge waved the longer line off with a loud "Thank you, everyone." Eight dogs were left — Breaker, McCreery, and Chicory among them.

"Do you think the judge recognizes McCreery?" Holly asked.

"How could he?" Nancy said, brushing an imaginary spot off her skirt. "McCreery hasn't been out in public for years. I imagine he's more curious about Benny."

One by one, the judge called out the eight remaining dogs and moved each one down, back, and around the ring. Benny was resting McCreery at every opportunity the way Bess had taught him. She sat rigidly on the edge of her seat and reminded herself to breathe.

When the last dog had finished, the judge walked

solemnly down the line. He paused when he came to McCreery, and a few people in the stands began to clap. Apparently indifferent to the applause, the judge continued his walk and waved Breaker, Chicory and Fandango forward. Jim and Breaker were at the head of the line.

"That's it for McCreery," Bess whispered when the judge ordered the five dogs in McCreery's line to circle the ring one more time. She figured he would wave them all off after this last chance to be seen. But no! As McCreery came around the last turn, the judge motioned him to the head of the short line in front of Breaker. With a wave, he dismissed the other four dogs. Bess could hardly believe her eyes. Her two poodles were in the final four and a third was McCreery's get.

Nancy gave a quick look through her field glasses. Flashes were coming from cameras all around them. "At least the judge will be able to keep them all straight: a brown, a white, a black, and a brown in a hunting clip shown by a kid. The photographers love it."

"He's moved those dogs seven times already," Holly shouted over the clapping. "McCreery couldn't look better if you were showing him yourself, Bess."

The judge called out McCreery for another turn around the ring. The drill was the same as before: down and back and once around in a circle.

"Easy, Benny. Easy, son," Bess warned in a whisper, knowing how excited he must be. In a million years, she never thought she would be in this spot. Breaker had the youth and vitality to go the distance, but her heart — and the crowd's — was pulling for McCreery.

"Look at that magnificent animal! It's taken generations to bring the breed up to that level," the announcer stage-whispered into his microphone. It was strictly against tradition, but nobody could do anything about it now.

Next came Breaker. Jim moved him around the ring like

they were floating, and then the whole performance was repeated with Chicory and Fandango. "I hope McCreery and Benny can hold out," Bess wished out loud.

Once more around the ring, and then the judge told Fandango and Chicory to step to the side. McCreery and Breaker stood alone in the ring, father and son.

The crowd cheered madly. Everybody knew they were watching the performance of a lifetime. Even the handlers who had been cut earlier clapped as the judge checked and rechecked the two dogs.

"Listen to that crowd. It's like they own stock in those two dogs," the announcer exclaimed with more than professional excitement.

"What a fabulous pair!" Hannah shouted over the din to anyone who could hear. Breaker had all the beauty of youth and generations of breeding behind him, but McCreery had the heart of a true champion and had stolen the affection of everyone in that great auditorium. When the judge moved him around the ring yet again, the announcer discarded the last of his professional composure and shouted, "I've never seen anything like it. Who are those dogs?"

"Either way, you've got a winner, Bess," Holly said. How could she say what everyone was thinking? Let it be McCreery.

Breaker's turn came again. He had never looked better. This was a great game to him, one he would love to win.

The judge called McCreery out again. "Take him down and back one more time," he ordered. Benny was holding himself together, his hunger to win written on his face, but the tightness around his mouth showed the effort he was making.

Holly stamped her foot. "What's the matter with that judge? Why doesn't he give it to McCreery?"

"McCreery's doing it all for you, Bess," Nancy shouted into her ear.

Benny signaled McCreery forward. The dog hesitated. Benny signaled again. McCreery trotted a few paces, stopped, shook his coat in place, and started again.

From where she sat, Bess could see Benny's mouth moving, speaking encouragements. They trotted a few more yards, and McCreery stopped again. He turned. For a long moment, he studied Breaker thoughtfully. Then he gazed across the ring into the grandstand and stared straight at Bess. He puffed out a sigh and sat.

Benny swung around in front and yanked on the lead, as if he could bring his vanquished hopes back to life. "Come on, boy. You can do it," he pleaded, almost in tears, but McCreery remained immobile with a powerful determination of his own. He looked into Benny's eyes and tapped his paw insistently as though begging him to understand.

Benny nodded. He walked McCreery out of the ring.

"Let's hear it for number nineteen, Champion Umpawaug McCreery!" the announcer shouted — breaking the rules again by announcing his identity. "Twenty-five hundred of the world's finest dogs entered today, one hundred and twenty-five breeds from every state, and I'm here to tell you, we've seen a dog here tonight with a heart so big Westminster will never forget him."

Bess rushed from her seat and onto the floor. As soon as he saw her, McCreery's tail began beating slowly. "Rrrrrr," he welcomed softly.

Bess reached around his neck and laid her cheek on top of his head. "Dear, dear McCreery," she whispered.

He wormed his head under her arm.

The hushed crowd burst into wild applause, and even the serene Nancy Valentine clapped until her hands were red. Over the roar of the crowd, the judge pointed at Breaker and yelled, "First!" but almost no one heard him.

"There are enough photographers on the floor to make

a major. Everybody wants a picture of that poodle," Bess heard the announcer say. "First time in Westminster history they've given the runner-up a standing ovation." The man was so beside himself, he almost forgot to tell his listening audience that Breaker had beaten a Picture Perfect Pete daughter for Best of Breed. By the time he remembered, Bess and Benny had led McCreery downstairs and out of the limelight.

CHAPTER 55

McCreery fell asleep on a padded dog nest as soon as they reached the grooming area. Benny and Bess sat on low folding chairs on either side of him.

Benny turned to Bess and said in a hoarse whisper, "McCreery gave up on purpose. I'm sure as anything."

"I know," she said, her voice coarse with emotion. "He's older than the other dogs, but he's healthy. He could have kept going."

Benny cocked his head. "Then why? He wanted to win. I could feel it."

Bess coughed, choking back her feelings. "No, he wanted me to win. Breaker had a better chance, so he yielded to youth. He gave me back the chance at Best in Show I lost the day I retired him early."

A roar so loud it reached downstairs informed them it was time for the Non-Sporting Group. Eighteen breeds as different from one another as a bulldog and a Lhasa apso would be judged against each other. Jim and Breaker would represent standard poodles.

Holly came rushing toward them from upstairs with a message from Jim. "You'd better go, Bess. Jim and Breaker are already lined up."

Bess studied the sleeping McCreery, a tangle of emotions written on her face. It would be foolishly sentimental to miss Breaker's big moment. His appearance in Group was probably the closest an Umpawaug poodle would ever come to winning Westminster's top prize, but didn't she owe it to McCreery to stay?

She waved a dismissive hand. "You go, Benny."

Benny and Holly glanced at each other furtively, as if they shared a secret. "You've waited your whole life for this, Bess," Holly said. "An Umpawaug poodle up for Group at Westminster! You've got to be there."

Benny straightened his tie and stuck out his chest. "I'll stay."

"Me, too," Holly added. "If anyone understands what this win means to you, it's McCreery. He's proven that tonight."

Bess still hesitated, like a cat approaching a puddle. As if to settle the matter, McCreery pawed in his sleep the way he did when it was time for a walk. She bent and ran her hand over his head. He breathed peacefully, barely stirring. She straightened up, tugging on the points of her shirt collar and pulling her jacket sleeves down over her cuffs.

Benny rocked on his heels and winked at Holly. If Bess hadn't been so preoccupied, she might have wondered why.

Time passed slowly, but finally the clamor overhead swelled again. Moments later, Bess appeared downstairs, gulping air. She started to speak, but the words wouldn't come.

Benny didn't need any. "I knew it! Breaker's going to be in Best in Show!" Benny shouted, flinging his arms against his sides.

Nancy Valentine hurried toward them. "Congratulations, Bess. Did you ever see anything like it? Breaker had the whole stadium in his hand. There would have been a riot if the judge hadn't picked him. CNN, Animal Planet, and all the foreign networks want interviews. Benny and McCreery, too. The four of you will end up on the cover of *Time*."

Benny pumped his hand in the air. "Yes!"

Holly turned to Bess. "You'd better go. The photographer's waiting, and they'll be calling for Best in Show any minute."

Bess signaled Benny to follow. She didn't need to ask twice.

The official photo only took a minute. The judge shook Bess's hand, then Jim's, and faded into the crowd. Overhead, the show steward called the Group winners to line up for Best in Show.

She reached into Jim's breast pocket and slid out the grooming comb. It was almost like he expected it. He nodded silently and handed her the lead. He shook hands with her, then Benny, and slipped away. Breaker stared up at her, still as stone, as if he knew the stakes were too high for foolishness. Benny was quiet, too, but he had to be wondering why she had sent Jim away and told him to stay.

To her, the answer was obvious. If it hadn't been for him, they wouldn't be waiting to go in for Best in Show. No longer a naïve, clumsy boy barely in charge of himself, he had matured into a first-class handler. He had faced and conquered every challenge she had thrown at him from Housatonic to Westminster. Didn't he deserve to take in Breaker for the most important contest of his life?

She no sooner permitted the thought than she shoved it away. She had worked her whole life for this moment. Benny was young. He would have other Westminsters ahead of him, wouldn't he? She deserved this one last chance, didn't she? The class wouldn't take long. She could manage.

Benny seemed to sense her discomfort. He stepped closer. "You're wondering who should take in Breaker, aren't you?"

Tears welled in her eyes.

He patted her arm awkwardly. "You should."

She gasped and tried to catch her breath. "Really?"

"Don't you get it? That's what McCreery was telling you when he sat down in the ring. He wanted you to win, even if it meant letting Breaker be the one who did it. That's how much he loves you."

A shudder ran up her spine as emotion threatened to overwhelm her. Benny reached to steady her, but she stepped back, signaling she was in control again. "You're sure?"

"Sure, I'm sure. My wish already came true tonight. I didn't tell you before, but my whole family is here. Together!"

She watched a warm flush appear in his cheeks and knew he was telling the truth. Her shoulders relaxed. "I'll do it."

"Good," he said, hitching up his pants. "I learned something from McCreery tonight, too. You don't have to come in first to be a winner. I'm going to find my own dream, like you found Westminster, and be a winner, too."

Her face grew dark, and she drew herself up to her full five feet. Breaker studied her with anxious eyes, uncertain what it meant. "Listen to me, Benny Neusner. You're a winner already. Other kids may be better at figuring out the area of an isosceles triangle or memorizing the capitals of Europe, but you're a first-class handler. No other boy your age has ever done as well."

He straightened the knot on his tie and stood taller. "I guess you're right. McCreery and I are winners, no matter who won the trophy." He rubbed his chin, considering, then broke into a smile. "Pretty good, huh? A poodle as jealous as McCreery letting Breaker get all the credit."

She looked fondly at the beautiful brown poodle beside her. "Pretty darn good."

She signaled with the lead and started walking toward the entrance to the great stadium. Benny followed alongside her. She wasn't going to change her mind; it just felt right to be together.

When they reached the spot only the dogs and their handlers could enter, he turned to her with a wistful look. "I wanted McCreery to be the one, but I'm not sorry it's Breaker." He squeezed the puppy's muzzle, careful not to mess up his coat. He hesitated, blushed, and leaned in to kiss her cheek. "Good luck, Bess," he said, and hurried off, as if on a mission.

Chapter 56

Breaker shook his coat into place and pawed the ground like a thoroughbred racehorse at the starting gate. Bess squared her shoulders, drew a deep breath, and headed for her place in line.

The other six Group winners were already lined up and waiting: the Standard Shnauzer for Working, the Gordon Setter for Sporting, the Smooth Collie for Herding, a Wire-Haired Dachshund for Hounds, a Fox Terrier, and the Japanese Chin for Toys. Each dog was a champion many times over. Any one deserved to be proclaimed the winner tonight.

The handlers of the smooth collie and the wire-haired dachshund made a space for her between them, and everyone, dogs and handlers, faced forward as on command. The buzz of anticipation grew in the packed stadium, and then suddenly, Madison Square Garden was plunged into darkness. A deep voice called out to the crowd. "Ladies and gentlemen, I give you the seven Group winners. Go ahead, clap your hearts out for your favorite."

A spotlight zoomed in on the entranceway, and a show official tapped the standard schnauzer's handler on the shoulder and urged him into the ring. The spotlight found him and the crowd erupted. Matching his pace to the dog's, the handler trotted around the ring, the glare of the spotlight tracing their once-in-a-lifetime journey. They came back to their marker to the cheering of the crowd, and the Gordon setter began his circle around the ring. The smooth collie followed. Bess whispered a reassuring word to Breaker and watched the setter complete her turn. The next moment she felt herself being pushed forward into the big stadium.

At first, the glare from the spotlight was so strong she had trouble taking in her surroundings, but as her eyes adjusted, they were powerfully drawn to the gold-and-purple medallion in the middle of the dark green carpet with the Westminster logo. "WKC" was emblazoned in purple letters tall enough to read from the uppermost bleachers. This was it! The spot she had aimed for all her life. Her heart was beating as if she had run a marathon. Westminster was everything she had dreamed of and more.

She licked the thin patina of sweat off her upper lip and circled the ring toward the seven gold markers for each of the seven group winners. A bouquet of yellow chrysanthemums stood beside each one. She halted when she came to the one with "Non-Sporting" written in purple letters. The spotlight left her and moved on to the wire-haired dachshund. She pulled out a comb and began touching up Breaker's coat while they waited.

In no time, the seven group winners were in place beside their markers, and once again, the spotlight returned to the entranceway. The announcer presented the judge over the P.A., and, probably like all the other handlers, Bess recognized her name. She raised toy poodles on the West Coast and had judged PCA in the past, but how would that play out tonight? Like the judges of the earlier classes, she was dressed in formal attire. Two show stewards dressed in tuxedos escorted her on either side, like double fathers in a bridal procession. Rosy sequins shimmered every time she moved, and no one could doubt this was a lady with definite tastes. She stopped at the judge's table, glancing at the huge purple-and-gold ribbon and the silver cups for the winner. Then peeling off the two stewards, she began her stroll down the line of markers, pausing momentarily before each dog.

The audience fell silent, as if in church. Even the peddlers hawking their wares grew quiet. Every handler was keenly aware of each flick of the judge's eyes, every muscle twitch. The dogs stood at attention, too, ears pricked, coats polished, eyes sparkling, feet ready to spring into motion. The judge's brilliant smile let everyone in Madison Square Garden know that a more perfect collection of dogs had never been assembled before in one spot. Then, her silent march over, she swung her hand out over the ring and signaled the dogs to circle once around.

The crowd came alive again with a roar as each of the seven Group winners passed in front of the judge. Bess caught a glimpse of the smooth collie, his short legs marching determinedly in front of her. She vaguely recalled hearing that this same judge had given him Best in Show once before in Tampa. The wire-haired dachshund was coming up behind her — a very good specimen of the breed, a dog everybody downstairs was talking about. The others followed in order until finally, even the tiny Japanese chin had found his marker again, and the judge signaled the standard schnauzer to come forward to be inspected.

Disappointed it wasn't his turn, Breaker tugged on his lead, prancing in place. Bess leaned in and whispered, "Be patient. It won't be long now."

A roar of approval erupted as the judge finished her hands-on inspection of the Working Dog and ordered the Gordon setter down to the end of the ring and back. The handler did a wonderful job of presenting her, but the judge must have noticed she broke a little coming back down. Tonight even one tiny flaw could make the difference.

She came around the ring and took her place again at her marker.

Bess kept all her attention on Breaker, willing him to stay focused on her. She hardly noticed what was happening a few feet away as the last dog before them, the smooth collie, circled the ring.

At last, the Non-Sporting winner was called, and she and Breaker stepped forward. The crowd fell into a watchful silence as the judge inspected Breaker from every angle. Jim had put him down perfectly, but so had the handlers of all the other dogs. Bess pushed the thought out of her mind and concentrated on the moment.

"Take him down and back," the judge ordered, pointing out the route the other group winners had taken.

The entire Madison Square Garden held its collective breath as Bess and Breaker turned to face the far end of the ring. This was their moment of destiny: hers, as well as his. "Here we go, big fella," she whispered, flexing her fingers. She took a deep breath and off they went. Even from the end of the lead, she could see he was breathtaking. All she had to do was keep up. He had never shown like this for anyone else — not once! He was giving his all for her, and the crowd knew it.

They reached the far end and pivoted to make the return. The crowd fell silent again. She would need to push herself a little now so Breaker could reach his full stride. She readied herself, head held high, and signaled him forward. A lightness came over her body as she stretched her legs out, toes hitting the ground delicately and springing back into the air. For a few magical moments, she and Breaker were moving together, in tune as experienced lovers. The wind sang in her ears, and then, suddenly, the music turned to gasps as she fell to the ground, pulling Breaker down with her.

The silence was deafening.

By the time Jim reached her side, Breaker was licking her face anxiously.

"Don't stand there," she snapped. "Help me up."

"Are you all right? Maybe we shouldn't try to move you."

"Don't be ridiculous. My bad knee went out, that's all. Being a damn fool's not fatal."

Jim helped Bess to her feet while everyone in Madison Square Garden, not to mention the millions watching on TV and webcasts all over the world, waited. As she took her first tentative step forward, the crowd clapped politely. Jim pointed to a folding chair someone had set up on the sidelines. "Here, sit," he ordered, easing her into it. She leaned back and closed her eyes.

Applause rocked the stadium, and she jerked into upright awareness. Apparently, she had dozed off. She turned in time to see the judge hand the standard schnauzer the heavy trophy. Jim was waiting beside her, but Breaker was gone. Presumably, someone had taken him back to his crate. She started to ease herself up. "Well, that's it. Time to round everybody up and head for bed."

Jim pushed her back gently. "Absolutely not. You sit here and rest. I'll get the dogs and bring you over to the Waldorf in our car. Benny's spending the night with his family, so you don't have to worry about him."

She was too tired to argue and grateful someone else was taking charge. Her whole body ached with fatigue and all she wanted was sleep. There would be time enough tomorrow for regrets, but not for second guessing. She had lost her chance for Best in Show through her own actions, but she had made the right choice. Umpawaug poodles made great champions because of their love for their owners, as McCreery had proven to the world tonight. She had acknowledged his gift by taking his son in for Best in Show herself, no matter the cost.

She must have dozed again because she was awakened by a voice blaring over the loudspeaker, summoning the dispersing crowd back to their seats. "Ladies and gentlemen, we have a special treat tonight. Westminster Kennel Club and the Poodle Club of America have joined together to present a special tribute. Dog lovers everywhere, I give you Bess Rutledge, the woman who has done the most to improve one of the most popular breeds in America."

A spotlight zoomed in on her, making dark spots jump in front of her eyes. Holding her hand up like a visor, she followed the spotlight to the far corner of the stadium. From out of the darkness strode McCreery, tremendously proud of himself, with Benny at the end of his lead. And that was only the beginning. Behind McCreery came two of his Best in Show get: Playing It Cool led by Felix and Tender Trap with Nancy Valentine. Close behind them came Holly and Jim with DandyLady and three more of McCreery's championship offspring, one in each hand, followed by two each of their champion puppies, and so on and so forth, all the way out to Hannah with Crumpet and Chicory, until, finally, where David would have been, Breaker brought up the rear alone. An Umpawaug pedigree come to life before her eyes. In the places where the dogs' names would be written stood the living, breathing animals — generations of fathers, mothers, and offspring — fanned out across Madison Square Garden like the family tree in the front of an old Bible.

The roar of the crowd grew to a crescendo as McCreery came to a halt at her feet. "Rrrrrur," he greeted.

"Sit," Benny ordered, but McCreery bounded up on his hind legs and placed his paws on Bess's shoulders. She wrapped her arms around his neck and pressed her nose into his coat. The lavender scent of the shampoo she had used to wash him the night before — a lifetime ago — filled her like coming home after a long journey. "You've done well," she whispered. She lingered a moment, the applause reverberating in her ears. Then she lifted McCreery's paws off her shoulders and urged him back down on the ground.

"You didn't have a clue, right?" Benny asked, a grin like a half moon lighting his face.

She looked up at him, his big frame dwarfing hers. For the first time, she noticed a little peach fuzz on his chin. His braces had vanished, too. "Not one."

"It was all of us. David, too."

Her eyes followed the spotlight as it moved back out into the ring where her friends stood waiting. Imagine them keeping a secret like that, especially from Mona. Her twin sister couldn't have known. She would have given the surprise away for sure. Thinking about Mona, she imagined that her sister *was* there, sharing in it, but the feeling flickered away as fast as it came.

"Laaadies and gentlemen," the announcer boomed again, "let's hear it one more time for Bess Rutledge and Umpawaug Kennels."

Benny puffed out his chest and found his place again at the top of the pyramid. This time he held McCreery in one hand and Breaker in the other. McCreery shook his coat back into place, and they were ready to go.

Bess raised her hand in a silent blessing as McCreery passed by, stretched to the end of his lead, head held high. In close pursuit, Playing It Cool and Tender Trap led the top half of the pedigree, while Breaker brought the bottom half safely home. Behind them, yards and yards of puppies fanned out across a ring as big as a football field. Sixty-five champion standard poodles, all coming down from McCreery.

It was a sight she would never forget, not as long as she lived.

Author's Note

ALMOST PERFECT grew out of my imagination during the dinners I was privileged to attend at the home of Dr. Sam and Mary Peacock during the Poodle Club of America's annual shows. This happened back in the 1970s, when PCA was an elegant affair held outdoors in the rolling hills of Pennsylvania. In addition to Mary and Sam, other legends of the poodle world included Wendell Sammet, Jackie Hungerland, and Rebecca "Beck" Mason. Over dinner, Beck and Jackie, encouraged by the others, described their dream of establishing a brilliant line of brown standard poodles. Their hopes were never realized in the flesh, but hopefully, the traits and beauty of the brown standards they wished to preserve are captured in McCreery and his offspring Breaker.

Like the dogs of the fictitious Umpawaug Kennels, all persons and events are the product of my imagination. Any resemblance to any person, living or dead, is purely coincidental. When a real name is used, such as Westminster or Poodle Club of America, the specific events described are fictitious and liberties were taken with details like dates and places to suit a dramatic purpose.

I have tried to be accurate in describing the way dog shows are run and points are won; any errors are unintended and the fault is mine. My apologies if I have offended any of the hardworking and devoted men and women who spend their time, money, and love breeding and showing beautiful dogs of all breeds. No disrespect is intended to the real dogs that actually participate in Westminster.

Many people helped in the writing and reviewing of this book. Chris Bulba, who accomplished the challenging feat of winning Obedience at PCA in 1992, gave me early encouragement. My fellow members of the Bluebonnet Poodle Club were also generous with their time and knowledge. Among this group, very special thanks go to Betty Johnson, a dedicated standard poodle breeder, and Sherri Smith, a skilled writer/editor and leading breeder of miniature poodles, who helped me traverse the technicalities behind the shows depicted.

Many others read various drafts of the novel, including author/illustrator Berthe Amoss, Renee Casbergue, Diane Hammer, MD, Susan Howard, Holly Guran McAlary, Millicent Neusner, Linda Siemers, Beth Willinger, Anne May and Barbara Skjonsby. The Magenta Writers Group in Ajijic, Mexico provided generous support: Marci Bowman, Nina Discombe, Margie Keane, Santos Lacy, Rachel McMillan, and Ada Robinson. Special thanks to Carol Gale Myers for her quick wit and enthusiasm. The Algonkian Group that met in Harper's Ferry with Michael Neff, the William Faulkner Pirate's Alley Society's Words and Music Festival, and Aviva Ehrlich, Robert Guinsler, and Eugene Winick all encouraged me when my book was in its early stages. Jeff Chalkley, DVM, provided veterinary expertise. Jennifer A. Valencia assisted with an earlier draft. Sally Asante brought her keen insight and good eye to a final edit.

My own standard poodles over the years, Miranda, Star, Mister, and now Miss-Tee, have taught me that poodles need love, care, space to run and human patience beyond the usual. They are sociable, high maintenance, and frequently naughty. They do not do well when left home alone all day. They are not ideal pets for everyone who wants a dog.

Almost Perfect
Book Club Guide

1. Benny's father believes dog shows are nothing more than "beauty pageants," more to show off the people than the dogs. In what way do the people and dogs in the book support or refute that opinion?

2. Benny's and Bess's ability to relate to their blood relatives is troubled. What enables this teenage boy and this seventy-year-old woman, with their different ages and backgrounds, to connect when their own parent/child relationships are so difficult?

3. Parents' expectations can influence the direction of their children's development. How did Benny's and David's parents' expectations affect them? Steffie's mother and Steffie?

4. Children like Benny are described as "special." What unique qualities compensate for his "specialness?"

5. Kate tells David that Benny must learn to accept his mother for who she is and not hope to change her. Is that good advice?

6. What explains the strong and immediate connection

between David and Benny?

7. Dr. Kate acknowledges she has her own problems in committing to a romantic relationship with David. How does this affect her professional ability to help others, including Benny and Bess?

8. Autistic children are described as being "on the spectrum," suggesting a wide difference in characteristics of children diagnosed with that disorder. The boy in *The Curious Incident of the Dog in the Night,* for example, is described as autistic and yet is different in many ways from Benny who fits the more inclusive criteria set out in the recent *Diagnostic and Statistical Manual.* Would it have been more helpful for Benny's dad to pay greater attention to his son's diagnosis? What about Steffie's mother?

9. What explains the attraction between Benny and Steffie? How do their respective strengths compensate for each other's weaknesses? They promise to love each other forever. Is that possible at their ages?

10. The relationship between adult children and their parents can be complicated. How is the relationship between David and Bess typical? Unusual? David disappoints his mother on the most important day of her life and stays with Kate instead. Was that the right choice? What does it say about his development over the course of the novel?

11. Even though Kate and David are not married, Kate and Bess seem to navigate some of the potential pitfalls for mothers- and daughters-in-law. How do they manage that?

12. The book takes place in the early 1990s. What would be different if the events took place today?

13. Bess and Mona disagree about the smallest things, yet have the profoundest love for one another. Why is Benny an exception, so that both women can agree about him? Are they "typical" twins? Does the fact that they are twins make them different from other siblings?

14. David and Bess credit Mona with nurturing David and helping him become the man he is. How unusual is it for a third party, whether relative, teacher, or friend, to make a significant impact on a child's development?

15. Steffie appears to have changed without the benefit of a specific therapist's or adult's help. Is the confidence she displays as she heads off to boarding school genuine? Have other "resilient" individuals in literature or life overcome difficult childhoods and even gone on to become super-achievers?

16. How does Bess's friendship with Benny permit her to do what she had wanted to do all her life but failed — make a try for Best in Show at Westminster?

17. At the end of the book, Benny's dad has changed his view of his son. How did that happen? Was Benny's success in the show ring the only reason?

18. Benny and Bess appear to be deeply affected by McCreery's unusual behavior at Westminster. Can a dog understand his owner so deeply that he would substitute his judgment for the handler's? Can an animal really alter a human's character?

19. Bess appears to be different by the end of the book, but can people really change at her age?

20. How does Benny's experience with McCreery and Breaker transform him? Will the change be permanent?

Diane Daniels Manning is a life-long lover of standard poodles. She learned the inner workings of dog shows and running a kennel by writing an authorized oral history of a lifetime president of the Poodle of Club of America who sold Diane her first poodle.

In her several former lives, she has been a teacher, a university professor, a child and adult psychoanalyst, and is currently the co-founder of The New School in the Heights, a therapeutic school in Houston. Her writing awards include the Faulkner-Wisdom Novella Prize and the Women in Film and Television Short Script Competition.

When not at The New School in the Heights, Diane and her writing partners, a Standard Poodle named Misty and a rescue cat named Elvira, convene at the keyboard to share great thoughts and plan the dinner menu.

Made in the USA
Monee, IL
26 May 2025

18173770R00157